DEVELOPING THE ART

OF EQUINE COMMUNICATION

For Joan

Enjoy the ride!

C. L. "Lee" Anderson

DEVELOPING THE ART

OF EQUINE COMMUNICATION

C.L. "Lee" Anderson

MOONLIGHT MESA
ASSOCIATES

WICKENBURG, ARIZONA

PRINTED IN THE UNITED STATES OF AMERICA

Published by:

Moonlight Mesa Associates, Inc.

18620 Moonlight Mesa Rd.

Wickenburg, AZ. 85390

928-684-5231/5235

www.moonlightmesaassociates.com

orders@moonlightmesaassociates.com

ISBN: 978-0-9827585-3-3

LCCN: 2012934999

Cover by Vin Libassi

Cover photo by Allen Patrou Photography

www.apatrouphotography.com

In Memory of...

Vern Danielson, a gentleman I rode with as a teenager. He was old enough to be my father, but we had a mutual respect for each other and were good friends. He was an Iowa farmer, a cowboy at heart, and a first class horseman. He's been gone for several years, and I miss him.

Disclaimer

Both the author and the publisher agree that *Developing the Art of Equine Communication* is meant for informational and educational purposes only, and is not meant as advice, instruction, or diagnosis of any particular problem relating to horses, horse training, common equine issues, or any other related or unrelated issues.

Neither the author nor the publisher assume any liability whatsoever to any reader or third party regarding any subject matter contained in or interpreted from this work, liability being expressly denied.

TABLE OF CONTENTS

Preface

Acknowledgements

The Magical, Mystical "Horse Whisperer".....1

The Invisible Third Party 9

Unintended Consequences.....17

Learning The Equine Language.....31

Sound Affects.....41

In the Eye of the Beholder.....51

The Physical Touch.....61

Something Smells.....71

Reward and Punishment.....77

The Art of Timing.....89

Muscle Memory.....101

What Nobody Talks About 117

The Bottom Line.....129

Horses That Have Helped Along the Way.....136

About the Author

Publisher Note

PREFACE

Anything elevated to a high science becomes an art form. Few would argue this. Few would also argue that a horse and its handler/rider performing in what appears to be perfect harmony and synchronization is an art form of a very high order. Since horsemanship involves both a horse and a human, the key to achieving this art form is communication between the two. Effective communication between two people is complex enough, let alone between a human (a predator) and a horse (a prey animal). To say this human/animal communication is complex is an understatement.

However, in no physical activity, including horsemanship, is it necessary to reach the extreme limits of perfection in order to thoroughly enjoy participating in the activity. Simply learning enough about horsemanship to ride with an acceptable measure of safety can provide countless hours of thorough enjoyment.

Quite a bit of what is covered in this book deals with achieving a high level of horsemanship. Please, don't let that scare you off. Even though you are dealing with a living animal, entry into the world of horse activity is not much different than any other physical activity. It involves a learning curve and the development of some level of skill.

A person's level of horsemanship will be limited to the level of communication they are able to establish with their horse. A good many people can be completely satisfied with equine communication at its most basic and simple level. A good comparison of this level of horsemanship against the "magical and mystical horse whisperer" level would be comparing the ability to ride a bicycle without holding on to the handlebars to participating in a national championship Bicycle Moto Cross (BMX) competition. As thrilling as that first time of letting go of the handlebars is, it is only a beginning. Of course, if a person never develops their cycling skills any further, there is still a lot of pleasure to be had from simply riding a bicycle. Look at your horse the same way. Learning to stay aboard and maintaining safe and positive directional control is only the beginning. Beyond this initial point, how far you want to develop your horsemanship in order to enjoy your horse is entirely optional. In today's world, many circumstances over which we have no control have a direct influence on how much of our time, effort, and resources we can afford to spend on developing a high level of horsemanship.

Regardless, the first and most basic step in learning how to effectively communicate with your horse under whatever circumstances your lifestyle might allow is to simply understand the nature of horses in general. Without this knowledge a person's horse experiences will always be lacking substance and their enjoyment will be limited. Even if you should happen to have the time, the abilities, and the resources and want to try reaching for the highest level of horsemanship, without a solid understanding of the nature of the horse you will never get to the level where your riding morphs into an art form.

I am often asked what to do about some particular horse problem. Seldom am I asked why the problem came about. If you understand enough about the nature of your horse, you won't need to ask anyone why it does or doesn't do something, or what to do about it.

And this, my friend, is why I wrote this book.

C.L. "Lee" Anderson
June 2012

ACKNOWLEDGEMENTS

I would like to express my sincere thanks to the following people for helping to make this book possible. First, I'd like to thank my mother, June Anderson, who has never doubted my abilities. Thank you, Mom. You know I love you. It is imperative that I thank my wife, Margaret, and my late wife, Donna, for their patience and tolerance above and beyond. I am grateful to Vern Danielson, friend and avid quarter horse man who actually admitted he admired my half Arabian.

I want to thank Paul Engelhardt, an honest-to-goodness old time cowboy, horseman, and friend. Without the support and encouragement from these people, this book would have been a more difficult project.

I would especially like to thank my good friend, Allen Patrou, for allowing his award winning photo to appear on the cover of this book. Allen's work can be seen at www.apatrouphotography.com. Listed below are just a few of Allen's accomplishments:

- Arizona's Photographer of the Year for 2012
- Arizona's Top Ten Photographer of the Year in 2006, 2007, 2008, 2009, 2011, 2012
- Recipient of the AZPPA Apple Award for Photographic Excellence 2011
- Recipient of the Kodak Gallery Award in 2008, 2009, 2011, 2012
- Arizona's First Place Open Portrait Division in 2007, 2008, 2011, 2012
- Arizona's First Place Open Commercial Division 2011
- Recipient of the Fuji Masterpiece Award in 2008, 2009
- Arizona's Third Place Open Portrait Division in 2009
- Recipient of Al Beuhman Trophy for 2007
- Recipient of Frank Rigo Award for 2006

DEVELOPING THE ART

OF EQUINE COMMUNICATION

ONE

The Magical, Mystical "Horse Whisperer"

Throughout history there have been tales of individuals upon whom Mother Nature appears to have bestowed a mystifying ability to communicate with horses. According to historical lore, horses don't just obey a "whisperer," the equines appear eager to please a "whisperer" and will perform the most amazing feats of cooperative obedience at a "whisperer's" gentle bidding. This ability to communicate in such a profound manner with a horse is simply a gift of nature bestowed on only a select few. What other explanation could there possibly be?

Well, I don't quite see it that way, and attributing this ability to Mother Nature doesn't exactly set very well by me. I've spent well over half a century of dedicated, serious study of horses: how and why they move, how and why they respond the way they do, and how to modify their behavior. Then along comes a person who hasn't, can't, or won't do what I've done, but because I'm able to accomplish things with this person's horse in minutes that his or her best efforts can't accomplish in any length of time, I am credited with being one of those natural "horse whisperers." I have to bite my tongue. They have just given Mother Nature credit for granting me some mystical power, and the years of dedicated effort I've spent diligently *learning* how to do what I do are written off. I'm very careful not to take offense, however, because I know the comment is intended as a compliment. Nature may have blessed me with a certain temperament, disposition, and maybe even desire, but I'd sure like my own efforts to get some credit.

I'm guessing the "horse whispering" myth came about because working with horses appears to be pretty straight forward to most people. If you kick a horse in the ribs, it goes forward; pull the left rein it turns left; pull the right rein it turns right; pull back hard on both reins and say "whoa" and it stops. If the horse is stopped and both reins are pulled hard, the animal backs up.

Of course, the first time a person climbs aboard a thousand pounds of equine with a set of lightning reflexes and a mind of its own, the rider is suddenly handed a very large dose of reality. The horse very quickly makes the rider aware that it doesn't necessarily see things the same way the rider does, and that it possesses enough raw power to do whatever it wants, whenever it wants. There is a sudden realization on the part of the rider that being astride this beast could prove to be very dangerous.

Then, one day this person happens to watch a high-spirited horse perform with flawless, artistic grace with minimal effort on the part of the rider. The horse actually appears to make an honest effort to please its rider. Horse and rider have an obvious bond and mutual trust. So, with a novice viewer's limited experience, and compared to the issues, incidents, and struggles the novice has had with his own horse, the only logical explanation he can come up with is that nature must have blessed this rider with some special mysterious ability to communicate with a horse; the rider must be one of those fabled "horse whisperers". What is not obvious to the untrained eye is that the performing rider is communicating *with* the horse, not dictating *to* the horse. There is a big difference.

Throughout the centuries horsemen have experimented with many methods of working with horses. Some methods were successful; some were not. Those methods that seemed most successful eventually evolved into a very loose and ambiguous set of practices that allowed most people to more or less "get along" with their horses. However, horses are not robots. Each horse is as different from the next as one person is from the next. Between horses and people, there are so many variables involved that a fixed set of "how to" rules is just not possible. This is why people today still experience the same equine behavioral issues people have experienced for centuries.

Due to its absolutely critical importance to a person's overall horse experience, the subject of horse communication is well worth some serious study, especially if a person hasn't "grown up" with horses and is entering the horse world as a "green" rider. Without proper communication skills, dealing with a horse is not just frustrating, it can be dangerous – sometimes dangerous to the point of being fatal.

Horses are large, powerful animals with absolutely no concern for human safety, feelings, or values. For anyone who says they've never been bitten, kicked, stepped on, thrown off or fallen off a horse, only one of two things is true: they've not spent enough time around horses, or they're not telling the truth. It's not a matter of what to do *if* these things happen – it's a matter of what to do to prevent them from happening, and what to do *when* they happen. Therefore, just as with any physical activity, it's a good idea to learn how to prevent bad things from happening. Only then is it possible to swing the odds in a person's favor when dealing with a rebellious horse. Of course, no technique is guaranteed to work every time on every horse.

When any given method of communication does not get the desired result, either the method was not correct or it was not applied correctly *under the circumstances at that time*. It baffles most novices when something that worked in one set of circumstances has little or no effect in a different set of circumstances. Invariably, the novice will blame the horse. The experienced horseman shrugs it off as the horse just being a horse. In this matter, there is no substitute for experience.

A common assumption is that the more complex an activity the more difficult it is to do. This is simply not true. A level of complexity is determined by the number of simple steps that are involved in successfully carrying out an activity. Moving 200 pounds of dead weight with nothing more than bare hands and brute force might be pretty difficult, but it's not a very complex process. Communicating with a horse is a very complex process, but each individual step is very simple. With horses, the issue of complexity arises out of the need to analyze and choose in a split second which of the many number of simple steps is required in a given situation and to apply it correctly. Communicating with horses is very simple in theory. Applying this simple theory, however, is when things can become very complex.

The key lies in how quickly and accurately a person can predict the results of applying a given method of communication under an almost endless set of circumstances. That might sound impossible, but it isn't. A major factor in this business of communication is the personality and temperament of both horse and handler, along with their level of trust in each other. Success can be drastically affected by what the horse may have already accidentally learned or been taught by other handlers. Books, like this one, can be a big help in learning theory, but there is only one way to learn application – and that is in spending many hours in field study and hands-on experience. It's very important to remember that if a person is going to continue doing the same things in the same way, the same results will ensue. This applies equally to both positive and negative results. Therefore, one must ruthlessly analyze what, why, and how one is doing with his or her horse.

I'm not a psychologist, but I have a notion that attributing someone with being a "natural" or a "horse whisperer" is an unconscious attempt to justify one's own shortcomings. It is a socially acceptable, plausible, and dignified explanation that sounds perfectly logical to others with the same shortcomings, thereby proving those shortcomings are really no one's fault. Mother Nature simply shortchanged them.

Thanks to the industrial revolution in the 19th century, everyday life is filled with electro-mechanical devices. Almost from the day a person is born, and on a daily basis thereafter, nearly everyone deals with machinery and electronics in some form. Automobiles, TVs, dishwashers, clothes washers and dryers, cell phones, and computers are as common as dirt. Even toys for two and three-year-olds are electronic, mechanical wonders. Very early on we learn that pushing buttons, pulling levers, and stepping on pedals will make these inanimate objects work for us and entertain us.

There is another aspect of modern life to which we are exposed from about the age of five. Since it is instilled in us during our mentally formative years, it is simply accepted that the only way to learn anything with any measure of success is to become educated. It is further accepted that the only way to get an education is to attend an "approved" school of some sort or to take lessons from a "qualified" expert.

Then, one day a person is introduced to the horse world. It is a world that revolves around large, intimidating, extremely powerful, non-electronic, non-mechanical animals that have personalities, likes and dislikes, and minds of their own. It quickly becomes apparent that horses have no concern for human wants, needs, or values, nor do they care in the least how much money or education one may have, or where one got it. All that matters to a horse is what is done with it, to it, and how the handler goes about doing it.

Ironically, electronic and mechanical devices actually do have something in common with horses. People are seldom interested in how or why devices function, only in how devices can *be made* to function. There seems to be a common assumption that learning the intricate details about how and why things function is far too complicated, takes way too long, and really isn't necessary, anyway. All that is really necessary is to know how to trigger the device to get the immediate result a person is after. *What button do I push? What lever do I pull and how hard? Which pedal do I push and how hard*?

One of the most common myths in the horse world is that any issues a person is having with his horse can be eliminated by sending it to a "professional" trainer. After all, if a person has issues with his automobile, computer, or dishwasher, he calls on a professional. The fallacy in sending the horse to a "professional" is that the issues for which a horse is sent to the professional are often caused by the owner and will more than likely return unless the owner/handler changes the way he does things with his horse.

There are methods by which it is possible to reduce a horse to a mechanical, almost robotic status. The animal is systematically broken down mentally, and any display of natural spirit or resistance is removed. Once this is done, it becomes pretty much a matter of what button gets pushed, what lever is pulled, and which pedal is stepped on. Of course, a horse handled in this manner is going to respond with the same glassy-eyed, detached, numb, and brain-dead lifelessness as any electronic or mechanical device.

Many horse people find the results of this form of "training" to not only be desirable, but assume it to be an extremely high level of training. They get the same sort of response from the horse they are used to getting from the electronic and mechanical devices in their lives, so they are very comfortable with it. Nothing happens any faster than they can think and react. They assume they are in total control, and they feel safe. However, to any *real* horseman, this is one of the sorriest, most pitiful and cruel results imaginable where the mental health of the animal is concerned.

For me, the most frustrating aspect of this common, sad state of affairs is that with just a little dedicated study, applied logic, and focused effort, nearly anyone can reach some level of soul-satisfying "horse whispering" and be working with a much happier horse.

Notes

TWO

The Invisible Third Party

It's commonly assumed (due to our technological advances) that anything done today is being done far better than it was ever done in the past. Where horses are concerned, however, close scrutiny reveals that this really isn't very likely. Underneath the façade of our modern high-tech, electro-mechanically advanced world, both people and horses are still the very same creatures of nature they were thousands of years ago. This means there is an invisible third party playing *the* key role in everything we humans attempt to do with a horse – Mother Nature.

Domestication of the horse triggered some of the most significant advances in human existence. Even with the invention of the wheeled cart, without the horse to pull the cart man was still limited by how heavy a load he could tote, and how far and how fast he could cover ground on foot. For centuries horses were the vanguard of military technology. This had a drastic effect on human history. Military conquests that would have been impossible otherwise were made possible because horses could move men and supplies farther and faster than ever before. Down through the annals of history, millions of mounted warriors' lives depended on their ability to efficiently use the natural abilities of the horse under the most extreme conditions and circumstances imaginable – the chaos of the battlefield. To think that only in modern, "enlightened" times have we finally discovered how horses should really be properly fed, trained, and cared for, strikes me as arrogance with considerable ignorance thrown in. Nowadays we may have a better understanding of the sciences of nutrition and medicine, but the mental processes of horses and humans aren't any different today than they were 3,000 years ago when the oldest known horse training manual was recorded.

Technological advances only change the equipment and methods now used, not how the brain *interprets and processes* information. When it comes to horses, any equipment or technique applied in exactly the same manner today that it was applied 3,000 years ago will produce the exact same results today that it did 3,000 years ago.

Horses have always been prey animals, and humans have always been predators. Predators eat prey animals. These facts dictate that a prey animal will have its guard up any time a predator approaches, and nothing can change these facts. However, we can learn how to effectively deal with these facts to our advantage. What is so often overlooked is that it is the human who has to do the learning, not the horse. We have the mental capacity, and the horse does not. A simple test that proves this is to turn an unmanageable horse loose in a small grass paddock with plenty of water. It may run around like a fool for a little while at first, but if left alone it will quickly go to quietly grazing, maybe doze a little in the shade, and in general take on the laid back demeanor of the average kid-broke, school horse...*as long as it is left alone*. But, just let a person attempt to catch the horse and it will immediately transform back into an unmanageable animal. Invariably the horse is faulted. The fact that there was absolutely nothing wrong with the animal's behavior until a human became part of the equation is curiously ignored. A horse does not have the mental capacity to react to any given situation in any manner other than what it deems is in its own best interests under the circumstances. I have to wonder if maybe that concept is just way too simple.

Very few things really cause horses much concern. They are largely concerned with eating, not getting hurt, and propagating. In a horse's natural state, eating is only a problem in extreme conditions. Horses are grazers, and they live where food is normally available. Their digestive systems are designed for low-powered grasses, a little natural salt and minerals, and water. In the wild, this business of not getting hurt is the key to a horse staying alive. While eating is an important factor in staying alive, horses are prey animals, and other natural survival instincts often take precedence over eating. A horse that becomes hurt or sick in the wild usually doesn't last long.

Humans tend to give little consideration to the fact that being born and raised in captivity in no way diminishes any of a horse's instinctive survival reflexes. Thousands of years of surviving have resulted in an equine social order that relies on safety in numbers, an untrusting attitude, an unbelievable awareness of surroundings, and a set of lightning-quick reflexes.

Horses are very timid animals. Without claws, fangs, or wings, their first line of defense is instant speed. Almost anything that makes a sudden sound or a quick move can trigger an instant "get outta here" reflex. Absolutely no thought is required. These reflexes were developed to keep them from being eaten. Under fear-induced flight, *any* form of restraint is blindly fought with all the fury that 1,000 pounds of muscle, hooves, and teeth can unleash, and no amount of domestication will ever alter this in the least. Interestingly, should a particular noise or movement occur often enough, even in the wild, without causing a problem for a horse, it soon learns to accept the sound or movement as normal and pretty much ignores it.

The natural urge to propagate is just as strong in a domestic horse as in a wild one and is the source of many conflicts and problems. In domesticated horses it often creates some very scary situations if not handled and dealt with correctly. There's more on this later.

So, what about human nature? Has it changed any over the last several thousand years? As much as we may like to think so, and as desirable as it might be to do so, the answer is no. And it isn't going to change, either. Underneath our slick "civilized" veneer, we're no different today than we were eons ago. We're still predators. We have always used natural resources in such a manner as to allow us to survive with less effort and reduced danger. We often meet aggression, perceived or real, with a show of force and bravado. It is also a universal human trait to assume that only in these modern "enlightened" times have we finally figured everything out and know how to do everything better than it has ever been done before. Funny how every generation thinks that, isn't it? So, it must have been just dumb luck that ol' Pythagoras happened to stumble onto all those algebraic theorems 4,000 years ago. Common sense tells us that without a PhD, a computer, or even a calculator, there's no way Pythagoras could've done all the complicated necessary mathematics to develop his theorem. He didn't even have a high school diploma! In the 1600s the well-known English philosopher, Sir Francis Bacon, once observed: "We think according to nature, speak according to rules, and act according to custom." Human nature is a lot more baffling than anything I've ever come up against in a horse.

Putting the opposite, natural worlds of horse and human in close proximity often results in a great deal of friction. When looked at out of context, the situation is almost ludicrous: imagine a 150 to 200 pound predator who's going to make this 1,000 to 1,500 pound prey animal lose its fear of him, and this predator actually expects this prey animal to just stand there and allow the predator to ride on its back and tell it what to do and when to do it. The simple act (to a person) of sitting on the back of a horse violates, to its very core, the deepest, natural survival instinct a horse has. Being on a horse's back is the optimal position of advantage for a predator to kill it. There isn't one sound, logical reason why a horse would ever allow this, but it does.

Some understanding of how horse and human minds work can explain how this comes about. A horse can't alter, adjust, or change its nature any more than it can fly. Neither can a human. However, both can make drastic adjustments in the way they interpret and respond to recurring situations. A human, with enough determination, concentration, study, and work can consciously alter his thinking to make it compatible with that of a horse. Conversely, a human can also learn enough about the nature of a horse and its natural reflexes to *force* it to perform certain actions. Both approaches work. The first approach works pretty well; the second one also works – sort of.

The first approach (consciously altering one's thinking to make it compatible with that of a horse) produces a trusting horse that has no fear or dislike of people, is pleasant to be around, has a real interest in and zest for life, is cooperative, enjoys its work and willingly performs its learned tasks to the very best of its ability. The second approach (using force) produces a horse that, though somewhat limited, performs well enough to get a job done. However, the horse does it grudgingly and under stress, doesn't trust people and avoids them whenever possible, tends to be rebellious and unpleasant to be around, exhibits little real spirit and never performs its best or to its handler's complete satisfaction.

It is the first approach that will be explored more deeply in the following chapters.

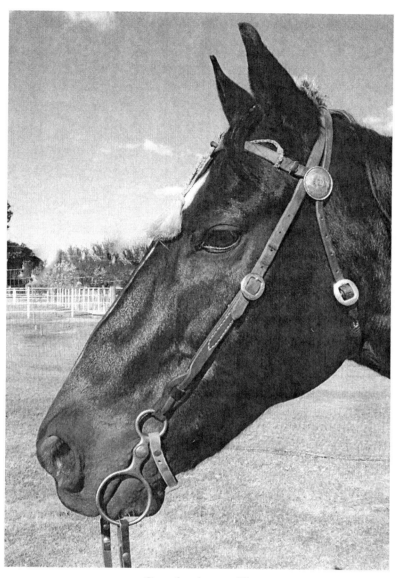

Concho in profile

(Photo by C.L. "Lee" Anderson)

Notes

THREE

Unintended Consequences

The phrase "unintended consequences" is usually associated with some piece of political legislation enacted with nothing but the best of intentions on the part of the lawmakers. Then their good intentions backfire due to some aspect of the legislation that was unintentionally overlooked, and the results are disastrous. This also occurs in the horse world, and it occurs more often than is realized. In the horse world these unintended consequences are often misinterpreted as open rebellion or intentional misbehavior on the part of the horse when, in actual fact, the horse is only responding according to its inherent nature. Before journeying too far into this subject, though, a little horse training history needs to be reviewed. Some of this information may be common knowledge, but a refresher won't hurt.

Horses are amazingly adaptable creatures. Mother Nature intended them to roam free on open, natural terrain. So, what do humans do? We enclose them in fenced pastures, smaller fenced paddocks and pens, even smaller box stalls, and unbelievably confining horse trailers. One must admit, considering the limited mental abilities of a horse, this calls for some pretty heavy-duty adapting on the part of the horse.

In Mother Nature's grand scheme of things, the original purpose of horses was as a food source for various predators, of which humans are one. Then, a few thousand years ago somebody discovered that not only were horses an excellent source of meat, but that their natural fear of humans could be overcome and their behavior modified to human advantage. Horses could not only learn to tolerate and trust people, they sometimes could go so far as to actually seek human companionship. It was learned that, if handled right, a horse would carry or pull heavy loads, and it would even allow a person to sit astride it to cover great distances faster than a person could travel on foot. This had to have been one of mankind's most significant, all-time breakthrough discoveries. This discovery ranks right up there with the wheel because it so drastically changed the way the entire civilized human world lived. However, just because the horse's manner of living has been drastically changed, doesn't mean a horse's natural survival instincts have been, or ever will be, altered in the least.

As is common with so many breakthrough discoveries, the first practical use of equine behavioral modification was as a tool of war, and horses remained the forefront of military technology for several thousand years. It is impossible to even begin to comprehend the level of communication a person has to achieve with a horse to engage in the chaos of the battlefield. Besides serving in battle, horses also became the primary power source for agriculture, construction, and transportation.

Over the centuries a horse's behavior has always been modified (or trained) through two distinctly different methods, both of which

18

work: method one uses physical *force* to make the horse respond; method two *teaches* the horse to respond. The less a person understands the nature and mental makeup of horses, the more likely he is inclined to use method one – force. The more knowledge a person has about the nature of the horse, the more likely the teaching method will be used. As stated, both methods work, but force only works to a limited degree. *Forcing* a horse to respond involves considerable use of actual physical force. The theory here is that this force establishes the trainer's authority in the horse's mind. Horses with enough spirit to refuse to submit to a trainer using force are usually labeled hopeless outlaws, considered untrainable, and are scrapped. For those that do give in to force, it is with a severely damaged spirit.

Most likely the military first discovered the advantages of the second method of training – *teaching*. Nearly all horses require a very limited amount of *force* in the beginning. However, the military learned that a horse would easily and quickly respond predictably to a consistent daily routine once it got past the initial instinctive fight-or-flight stage. By using a rigid military routine, working quietly and maintaining calm, the horse would learn to respond predictably, *and riders would learn to communicate predictably.* Since all the horses and troopers were working to the same routines and using the same commands and methods, any trooper could be mounted on any horse and the two would be able to function as an effective team in the field. Both horses and riders also retained the lessons for the rest of their lives. This was an invaluable asset and undoubtedly a determining factor in the outcome of many a battle. This also became the foundation on which nearly all of today's formal equitation is based.

Then, in the middle of the 19th century the industrial revolution and the development of machinery drastically reduced the need for horses as a military tool, an industrial and agricultural power source, and a means of transportation. As a result, for all practical purposes the need for live horsepower became obsolete by the middle of the 20th century. As the horse's significance to, and influence on human accomplishment faded, so did much of the horsemanship that had been painstakingly learned over the span of centuries.

This knowledge was lost because it had been nearly always handed down by word of mouth. Precious little was ever documented. Until the end of the 19th century, the documentation of anything was done by hand with quill and ink, a time-consuming, labor-intensive undertaking. Few people were literate enough to do this scribing, and for those who were, there were other subjects considered far more important than horse training. And even if equine training had been documented, few people (even many of high social or political status) were educated enough to read.

By 1900 the industrial revolution had produced the mechanical printing press and mass documentation was born. Education became far more common and illiteracy was drastically reduced. In the 20th century the electronic revolution produced unbelievable technological and mechanical advances that served to drive the need for horse knowledge even further into oblivion. Now, in the 21st century, a few dedicated horse people are beginning to realize how much horse handling knowledge has been lost and how valuable it was.

Today the ability to read is common, and there are literally hundreds, if not thousands, of books printed about horse health, care, riding, and training. However, if even two million more horse books were to be published, there is one thing that cannot and will not change:

Horsemanship cannot be absorbed from a book.

For example, suppose you can't swim but want to learn. So, you set about educating yourself by reading everything you can about swimming. However, no matter who you are, how well your parents can swim, where you came from, how much education you have, or how big your bank account, sooner or later you have to get in the water, and the first time you go completely underwater not one word of what you "learned" from all your research will be remembered or be of any use. It's no different the first time a horse spooks and bolts, suddenly drops its head and goes to bucking, cow-kicks as the cinch is pulled tight, or any one of a million other things that horses can and often do.

The single, most important concept that is seldom considered when handling horses is that a horse is incapable of mentally projecting itself into the world of human values and ways of doing things. If, and *only* if, you can gain enough of a horse's confidence and trust will it allow you into its world. Until that happens, you cannot experience real equine communication, the deepest and most satisfying relationship a person can have with a horse. Only when you have gained a horse's confidence and trust will it respond to you in a cooperative manner of its own free will. Resign yourself to the fact there is only one way this will ever come about: you have to learn to communicate *with* the horse on its level, in its language. Dominating a horse through force has never been very successful because it nearly always triggers a physical confrontation. When things deteriorate to that level, the horse usually determines the outcome.

By definition, communication is the *exchange* of information. Therefore, the key to modifying the behavior of a horse hinges on a person's ability to communicate *with* it, rather than dictate *to* it. If information doesn't flow both ways, it isn't communication – it's dictation. And when dealing with a horse there is no better way to guarantee an unintended consequence than to be dictatorial. If you are not aware of, or sensitive to, what your horse is telling you, don't expect it to be aware of, or sensitive to, what you are telling it.

There are some major stumbling blocks when it comes to communicating with a horse. First, in horse "language" various *sounds* have definite meanings. Human words are nothing but sounds to a horse. The dictionary definition of a word means nothing to this animal. Volume, tone, and inflection are what a horse hears, and consistency is what it responds to. I'm well aware horses *appear* to respond predictably to a number of individual words uttered by a rider, but this doesn't mean they are responding to the dictionary meaning of those words. They are merely responding to a specific sound uttered in a consistent manner in a specific circumstance. The same word uttered in a totally different context, under totally different circumstances, or even in a different tone of voice, means nothing. If you think not, consider a horse that will, with no resistance, come to a halt whenever a rider gives the "whoa" command. However, when trying to catch that same horse, the same person roaring "WHOA" will more than likely cause further evasive action on the part of the horse. This is a classic example of an unintended consequence.

Equine mental capabilities are simply not sophisticated enough to grasp language. Therefore, one of the first things a person needs to do is to forget about expecting a horse to give a predictable response to the *meaning* of a spoken word, especially "WHOA!". No horse has ever been born knowing what that word means, but that is what is loudly yelled when a horse spooks. Any equine response to a word is going to be according to the circumstances, the volume, and the tone of the human voice, not the meaning of the word.

The major stumbling block to learning to communicate with a horse is that, for many legitimate reasons, few people today are willing or able to spend the time and effort required to learn the horse's language.

Horses are very timid prey animals with limited defenses and are instinctively aware that humans are predators. Horses' only defenses are running, kicking, and biting, and in that order of preference. Running is always their first line of defense. In a natural setting, unless and until *they* have satisfied *themselves* that a situation or an object is not going to harm them, their survival instinct tells them to escape from the threat as fast as *they* deem necessary and to stay at what *they* consider to be a safe distance from it.

Kicking is a limited option for a horse because kicking is strictly a close-quarter defensive action, and a horse has to be uncomfortably close for the kick to be effective. A horse has to be even closer to bite. This means that *any time* a horse becomes frightened, confused, or hurt, its immediate and sometimes violent reaction is to "get the hell out of there" at all cost. This doesn't mean that in a domesticated state a horse can't learn that the threat of kicking or biting can work to its advantage. A good many learn just that, and it is one of the major issues people have to deal with. What this all boils down to, is that if you don't learn how to communicate with your horse, you cannot modify its behavior to a consistent, predictable, and acceptable level.

You do need to understand and fully accept that your horse will, *without exception*, always respond to any action you take and any sounds you make, according to its interpretation at the time. Your intentions mean nothing. This is what unintended consequences are all about.

Now we can seriously address the subject of unintended consequences. You don't have to be around horses very long before you'll see someone attempt to sooth and quiet a frightened, nervous, or upset horse by stroking its neck or shoulder and crooning over and over, "Easy boy, easy…it's alright…whoooa now, easy, easy…." You'll also learn it isn't at all unusual for the situation to rapidly escalate to the point where the horse finally explodes, usually with disastrous results. Why did the horse not pay attention to what the rider was trying to tell it? First, the horse didn't understand the meaning of the words, and second, more than likely the person was just as scared and nervous as the horse. The horse doesn't realize the person is scared because he or she fears what the horse is capable of doing. All the horse knows is that both of them are scared, and the horse doesn't question but what it is for the same reason. The person may not have been at all afraid of what upset the horse, but everything the person communicated to the horse through actions and words was that there was something to be afraid of. The horse instantly picked up on this through the tone and inflection in the person's voice along with the nervousness in the hand stroking the neck. If the person had been mounted, his legs would have at least tensed if not actually gripped the horse's ribs. This is especially true if the rider was attempting to keep a secure seat. Everything about the way the person spoke and moved relayed to the horse that it really needed to be scared, and that it better get out of there.

24

The horse immediately and very accurately communicated to the rider what its intentions were. The rider's *intent* was totally misinterpreted by the horse. In a split second the horse's logic went something like this: (1) I'm scared; (2) the person is scared; (3) panic. The person fully understood this and began desperately trying to restrain the horse, which only served to increase the animal's fear. In a natural herd environment if anything scares one horse and it panics, not one of the others will question it, and they all instantly panic. In the final analysis, a scared horse with a scared handler is going to trust its own instincts and act accordingly. It also has the raw, physical power to do it. This is a perfect example of an unintended consequence triggered by the person.

You might wonder how a person communicates with a horse in a situation like this. If this is the question that came to mind, you haven't been paying attention. Most definitely the person *was communicating* with the horse, just not in the way the person thought. The fact of the matter is that as long as a person's only consideration is his own physical safety, there is little chance beyond dumb luck the situation will be resolved in the person's favor. I would suggest that instead of waiting until being thrown off the horse, a person dismount as quickly as possible. He may very well have to walk home, but at least he would stand a better chance of being able to do so. If in a group, the dismounted rider might then hand the reins (or lead rope) to someone with enough experience and confidence to handle the situation. A confident, experienced person's calm demeanor can often quickly communicate to the horse that the person is not afraid, which results in a much better chance of the horse calming down. In a situation like this, whether the outcome is acceptable or not depends entirely on the manner in which the person handles the situation.

Here's another source of an unintended consequence. Have you ever watched someone encourage a horse to run around in a paddock, an arena, or a round pen? This is common when showing off a horse's action to friends or relatives, maybe working off a little excess energy, or just admiring the way the animal moves. What is seldom considered, though, is that by doing this the person is actually teaching the horse how to run away and evade them. How is the horse supposed to know the difference between this innocent act (by human interpretation) and when the person wants to catch it? The horse will only have been very effectively taught how to evade people and will likely assume that's what is wanted. Completely unintentional, I know, but pretty darned effective, nonetheless.

When the person is finished with chasing the horse around and wants to catch it, the horse may keep evading him. If this goes on for a while, it tends to make the person angry. The longer this continues the angrier the person grows, and the angrier the person becomes the louder he'll yell "COME HERE!" or "WHOA!" (along with a few choice expletives) and the faster and farther away from him the horse tries to run.

Consider how you would instinctively react if a snarling, snapping, lip-curling pit bull approached you in an obviously aggressive manner. Every nerve in your body would be screaming, "Get the hell out of here as quickly as possible!" If another person were to come toward me, obviously angry and yelling in a language I didn't understand, I'd want to stay away from him, too. The logic behind purposely chasing a horse one minute then expecting it to allow itself to be caught in the next, escapes me. Regardless, it is a common occurrence. We've all witnessed it, and at one time or another most of us have even been known to do it, haven't we? When

26

the horse is finally caught, it isn't at all uncommon for it to be punished for running away. And what do you suppose the horse learns from that?

Over half a century ago a very wise horseman told me that what I taught my horses wasn't going to be nearly as important as what I didn't allow them to learn. Since nothing is ever unlearned (human or animal), I see no gain in purposely teaching a horse how to run away from me.

Let's apply some logic to this problem of catching a horse. Why wouldn't a horse, a prey animal, want to escape as far away as possible from an obviously angry, snarling, roaring predator – in this case the person trying to catch it? The person simply wants to catch the horse, but everything the horse hears, sees, and has experienced is telling it to run away and stay away; another fine example of an unintended consequence. Human body language and tone of voice often communicate a far different message than intended, and a horse will always assume your actions and tone convey your intent.

What has just been described are some common examples of the way many people unintentionally communicate with their horses and why the unintended results occur. In each of these examples the horse's interpretation was the exact opposite of the person's intent, and what the person thought should have been a very predictable response wasn't. It cannot be emphasized enough that your horse, *without exception*, will always respond to everything you do and the sounds you make according to *its* interpretation – not your intent. The response you receive tells you how your actions were interpreted. Start analyzing whether you are communicating *with* your horse or *to* your horse, because there is a world of difference between the two. Start looking at what you say and do from the mentally simple perspective of your horse, and you will find yourself dealing with issues in an entirely different manner and experiencing a lot more *intended* consequences.

Outside of a few outlaws that have learned (been taught?) how to effectively rebel, if your horse doesn't perform the way you want, you are either asking it to do something it physically can't do, or it doesn't understand what you are asking. In either case, it is not the fault of the horse. People are good at assuming they are telling a horse one thing when they are unintentionally telling it to do another, and then punishing the horse because it did the wrong thing. Then we wonder why we have "issues" with our horses. When it comes to horses, poor communication is so common it is almost the norm. Nowhere is the adage "actions speak louder than words" more true than when dealing with horses.

Many years ago Vern Danielson, an Iowa farmer, a good friend, and one of the few real horsemen I've ever known, once told me that he figured most horses do what they do in spite of their training, not because of it. Vern was right.

Can your horse be safely approached?

Notes

FOUR

Learning the Equine Language

Have you ever watched two people who didn't speak or understand the same language try to communicate? If so, my guess is that it was quite an entertaining exercise in charades with a lot of arm waving, pointing, very slow and clearly enunciated words, and the less success the people had trying to communicate, the louder they spoke. Regardless, if both parties were making an honest effort there was probably a fair degree of success. But, if either one of them had no desire to communicate, the attempt was a miserable failure. There is only one way to ensure success in this sort of situation – one of them has to learn the other person's language. This is precisely what many people are up against when attempting to communicate with their horses.

Horses do not have the mental capacity to learn human language even if they wanted to. Only if you can learn the horse's language is the horse going to listen to you or attempt to communicate with you in any manner, except maybe to let you know to leave it alone, which it will very effectively do by using the equine equivalent of the waving of arms, pointing, and even possibly getting loud. You won't have any trouble at all understanding what it is telling you. With ears flat against its neck, its nose pointed at you in a straight line with its neck, and its mouth wide open and roaring like a lion, no interpretation is required. Every square inch of the horse's body language will be communicating loudly and clearly: Back Off! Human or animal, intense anger and acute fear are expressed in a universal language. So are other emotions such as apprehension, pleasure, or confusion. But these emotions are often expressed in such a passive and subtle manner by a horse that people regularly misinterpret or ignore them.

So, where does a person go to learn this equine language? Go to the same place you would go to learn anything that cannot be documented. Go right to the source: in other words, horses. Before doing that, though, you're going to have to adopt a 180 degree shift in your mental attitude. You will need to resign yourself to being an ignorant student and give horses the respect they deserve as teachers. There will be no interpreter, no textbooks, and no final exams. Failure on your part will simply result in a horse experience that is not only frustrating, it can (and probably will) cause you some degree of embarrassment, and possibly even physical pain. So, if you really want to learn, be prepared to study diligently with a greater purpose than simply sitting astride a horse as a passenger.

Begin by finding a herd of horses that is loose in a good-sized enclosure. It makes no difference what breed, type, or size the horses are, and the larger the herd the better. The object is to observe how horses act and react toward each other in a natural herd environment. Watch very closely how they communicate amongst themselves. This is where and how the learning is done. Don't think it's going to be accomplished in one or two lessons, either. This needs to be an ongoing study for as long as you have anything to do with horses.

Once you've found some horses to observe, pick a spot that allows you to observe them unnoticed and watch them for an hour or two without doing anything to influence or interfere with their normal activities. It will take some time, but if you watch closely you will learn that many things people normally consider insignificant (if even noticed at all) are quite often very significant to a horse. Before long you will begin noticing a consistency in what they do, how they do it, and when they do it. Also, watch closely how one horse will react to what another is "saying" to it. You will learn to tell whether a horse is asking, telling, or questioning. You can even tell when they are confused. What may at first appear to be nothing more than the casual flick of an ear, the lifting of a foot, the swish of a tail, or the rapid raising or lowering of the head can be very significant. Take notice of not only how, but where they touch each other. Listen to the sounds they make and the results of these sounds. One horse simply turning to look at another can instantly transmit a very clear and definite message.

Once you start noticing these movements and the circumstances under which they occur, you can often predict what the message is going to be, when the message is going to be sent, and the response to the message. You will learn that the group has a definite pecking order. You will learn that, no different than a group of people, some horses are bold and aggressive, some are timid and passive, some are lazy, some are playful, some appear mentally sharper than others, some are more physically coordinated, and some are just plain unpleasant and even a little mean.

Determining a horse's natural personality is far more important when communicating with it than is commonly realized. Physically punishing a horse for being timid only creates fear in the animal and triggers its survival instincts to run away and stay away from you. Physically punish a bold and aggressive horse, and you might have a real fight on your hands. In both of these cases the horse's response is simply a perfectly normal reaction according to its personal nature.

You will also learn that a horse's reaction to any new or unexpected sight, sound, or touch is unbelievably quick and can be quite violent. This is because horses instinctively assume anything unfamiliar or out of the ordinary is a possible threat to their safety, and their survival reflexes have a hair-trigger. You'll also notice that if one horse suddenly "jumps" or "spooks," they nearly all do. They will at least come to attention and take notice. They never question, but react as though a threat to one of them is a threat to all of them. You will learn that any fear-induced response is often unpredictable and invariably lightning-quick. Their brain just shuts off and they react in blind panic. Whether they run away or attack depends entirely on how the fearful horse interprets the situation at the time. What you might think would be the most logical course of action has absolutely nothing to do with how a horse in fear for its safety, founded or unfounded, might respond. You will also find that horses have a lot of curiosity. Once they are far enough away and their initial fear subsides, they will usually investigate anything even the slightest bit unusual – unusual to them, *not to you.* It may very well be from what *they* consider a safe distance at first, but they still have a very strong desire to satisfy their curiosity.

You may be wondering what all this has to do with how you want your horse to respond to you under saddle. A fair enough question. When studying horses in their natural state, you will notice that their response to any stimulus takes one of only two basic forms: predictable or unpredictable. If you've watched closely enough, you will have also noticed that certain types of stimuli always produce a predictable response, while other stimuli will nearly always produce a very unpredictable response. If, when you are riding, you insist on doing the type of things that produce unpredictable responses from your horse, you can't expect a predictable performance from it. To be physically punished for any natural response, predictable or unpredictable, will invariably trigger the fight-or-flight instinct.

Most people, at least to some degree, eventually learn how to tell a horse pretty much what they want it to do, and most horses, at least to some degree, eventually learn pretty much what their riders are asking them to do. However, *every move* a horse makes *should* be telling its handler/rider something, and every move a handler/rider makes, intentional or not, *is* telling the horse something. This is called communication. Whether it contributes to the interactive experience in a positive or a negative manner depends on how each party interprets and reacts to what is being "said."

Give your horse credit for the fact that it is a living, responsive, feeling being. Just like you, the horse has fears, wants, needs, likes, and dislikes. If, whether on purpose or in ignorance, you pay no attention to these things, the horse often just quits trying to tell you anything, suppresses any show of spirit, and resigns itself to being little more than a brain-dead slave. It's not much different than you expressing your wants, needs, or ideas to your supervisor and having him routinely ignore you or, worse yet, punish you for expressing them. In the interests of self-preservation, you have only two choices: rebel and get punished (and maybe fired) or just shut up and adopt a "why bother" attitude and do nothing more than whatever it takes to get through to quitting time. Why people think this doesn't apply to horses escapes me.

35

If a horse consistently receives inconsistent or unfamiliar signals from its rider, it will eventually go pretty much numb when ridden. Many of us have experienced this in a rental horse. Its riders are seldom experienced, and no two riders ever do anything alike. The horse finally learns to just shut-off its brain, follow the horse ahead of it, and pay no attention whatsoever to its rider. It never knows if what its rider is doing is a signal to do something or not. If a horse is consistently blind-sided with unknown or unexpected actions from its rider, and these actions are applied with force, the horse doesn't dare relax and will be in a constant state of nervous anxiety. You would be no different in that respect. A horse can also be driven into a robot-like trance by being monotonously drilled in a limited number of specific actions until it becomes mentally numb. This is common in show horses.

Study the interaction of two or more horses closely enough and you will begin to understand just how sensitive they are to the meaning of the slightest move on the part of another horse. They can be just as sensitive to the slightest move on the rider's part. The problem is that the rider needs to be just as sensitive to the horse *as another horse would be.* This is where most people fail when it comes to communicating with their horses. The more sensitive you become to your horse, the more sensitive it will become to you. Communication is not a one-way exercise and, as the intelligent (?) half of the team, it is your responsibility to not only initiate communication, but to nurture it and build it. Only if you are able to "speak" to your horse in its language will it allow you into its world. If it will not allow you into its world, the two of you will always have issues that prevent a completely satisfactory relationship for either of you.

All species on earth have some unique means of communication that is understood by other members of the same species. Any horse can effectively communicate with any other horse anywhere in the world. It's the same with every living animal except humans. We had that ability eons ago but have since pretty much erased it through the development of language. Today, humans tend to assume nearly all communication has to involve words with dictionary meanings. What is often overlooked is that although sounds (not words, but *sounds*) in a limited form can be an effective form of communication, they are probably the least used of the four basic ways all horses communicate. The four methods used by horses to communicate are audible (sound), visual (sight), physical (touch), and one that people almost never consider because civilization has so dulled it: odor (smell). Whether applied purposefully, and whether applied by *either you or your horse,* these four forms of communication will have an effect.

Tone of voice will have more of an effect on a horse than the meaning of the words uttered, and your mental state at the time of utterance has a lot to do with the tone of your voice. No matter what you say or how hard you try, you're not going to fool a horse into thinking you are unafraid when you are actually scared witless. Some of the sounds horses are capable of making will curdle your blood and, if directed toward you, most assuredly will create acute anxiety.

With its eyes located at the sides of its face, a horse can easily see what its rider is doing. Sitting astride a horse you have a bird's-eye view of the most expressive part of a horse's anatomy: its head and ears.

If you think a horse cannot smell anxiety or fear in a person, you are badly mistaken. Fear causes a natural occurring odor over which you have absolutely no control, and a horse's sense of smell is exceeded only by that of dogs, and not by much.

Through the bit, the way the reins are held, the legs positioned, and posture in the saddle, a horse is constantly being fed an unbelievable number of messages. Conversely, a pricking of the ears, stiffening of the jaw or neck, a tensing of the back muscles, or a swish of the tail can send a rider an unbelievable variety of messages. It's just that most riders don't realize that even the slightest move they or their horse makes has the *potential* for being a significant message to one or the other of them. Of course, if neither one of them has any idea what the message is supposed to mean, the relationship will leave a lot to be desired. The inability to understand each other can very quickly degenerate into either a brain-dead nothingness or escalate into a 9-1-1 disaster. In either case, it won't be the enjoyable experience it could be for either horse or rider.

Far too many horses and their riders are not unlike two people who don't speak the same language (horse and rider) traveling in a boat down a white-water river (a trail ride). Only one of them (the rider) knows where they are supposed to be going and why. The other person (the horse) is only supposed to be paddling the boat and following orders. If the trip is to be completed without any serious negative incidents, an industrial strength amount of D-A-L (Dumb-A**ed Luck) will be required.

The following chapters will explore these four basic methods of communication. I guarantee that a solid understanding of them will have nothing but a positive effect on how you and your horse get along with each other.

Concho telling Lee a thing or two!

(Photo courtesy of Allen Patrou. Apatrouphotography.com)

Notes

FIVE

Sound Affects

Read the title of this chapter again. Take special notice that it says "sound" not "words," and "affects" not "effects." This is because almost any sound one makes can affect the sort of response one receives from a horse. Conversely, any sound coming from a horse can have a significant meaning. The bulk of communication between humans involves an understanding of the meaning of whole words. We seldom consider what those words actually sound like to a horse.

Words are complex collections of several different and separate basic phonetic sounds. Many words are a collection of individual groups of sounds called syllables. How a word is pronounced, some slight inflection, or the context in which it is used can totally change its meaning. The delicacies of spoken words are far too sophisticated for a horse to understand. For example: the word "whoa" is commonly uttered when a rider wants his horse to stop. It is also commonly used to slow a horse down. It's also a pretty common expression of surprise. How is a horse supposed to know which meaning is intended? The horse interprets whatever comes out of a person's mouth as nothing more than sound. Only when a particular sound is uttered in exactly the same volume, tone, and circumstance can a horse associate it with performing a specific action.

Just because a horse responds to a given word in one set of circumstances has nothing whatsoever to do with how it will respond to that same word in a different set of circumstances. Its brain simply cannot grasp the concept of a word (or a sound) having the same meaning in two or more different situations any more than it can grasp a word having two different meanings in similar situations. This also means a horse can learn to respond in a predictable manner to any sound, whether it is a word or not, as long as that exact same sound *means exactly the same thing under exactly the same set of circumstances every time.* When one considers the infinite number of situations and circumstances that can be encountered when handling a horse, and the fact that the horse does not understand the meaning of a given word, it is unrealistic to attempt to teach a horse to respond entirely to words. Even if it was possible to come up with that many different sounds, it's even more unrealistic to expect a horse's simple brain to remember all of them.

This doesn't mean audible cues have no place in the training of horses. It just means they should be used judiciously. Audible sounds should be reserved for only a few simple, basic actions by the horse. Although some horses will learn to respond to a multi-syllable word, a voice command is the most effective when it is one syllable and used in partnership with, or to reinforce, a cue that is seen or felt by the horse. This is still a bit tricky in that it isn't easy for a horse to focus its attention on more than one thing at a time. If the rider gives both a word command and a physical cue, whether or not the horse responds predictably depends on several things being rigidly consistent: timing (does the word or the physical cue come first?); volume, the horse's state of mind at the time, and even the rider's state of mind at the time. This is especially true if the same verbal command is used in conjunction with different physical commands. This will, in fact, only serve to thoroughly confuse a horse.

When a horse and its handler are truly communicating with each other, what a novice observer sees and hears can be misleading to the point of being dead wrong. To impress an audience, but more often than not done unconsciously and even unknowingly, it is common for many trainers to do what magicians and con-artists routinely do on purpose. They steer the viewer's attention in one direction while the significant action takes place somewhere else. For example, I've taught my horse Concho to smile. He sticks his nose in the air and curls his upper lip *ala* Mr. Ed. (For you younger readers, Mr. Ed was a popular TV horse program in the mid-1950s.) I started out by gently tickling Concho's upper lip with my index finger, and when he'd wiggle it a little he got a treat. Pretty soon all I needed to do was point my finger at his nose and that lip would start moving. Over a period of a few months his "smile" training progressed to where, without raising my hand above my belt, he would "smile" if I even moved my index finger. Just to emphasize how subtle a cue can be and how sensitive a horse can be, he only responds when the left index finger moves. When we are entertaining a group of people, I will ask Concho if he could show the folks how much he appreciates their presence by giving them a big smile. Immediately, everyone's focus shifts to his mouth and he smiles (in response to my *left* index finger moving which, with my thumbs hooked over my belt, no one sees). It is assumed he responded to what I asked. Magicians and con-artists refer to this as "bait and switch," and it works beautifully.

A classic example of this is when a nationally acclaimed horse trainer conducting one of his seminars is sitting on his perfectly trained horse in front of an audience that has considerably fattened his bank account. He tells the audience, "The key to keeping a horse under control is the ability to bend its neck, like this," and he proceeds to have the horse, with no resistance whatsoever, swing its head from left to right at what appears to be merely a feather touch on the reins. What he said, the words that he spoke, immediately shifted the audience's focus from the trainer to the horse's head and neck. The audience only saw what happened at the bit end of the reins. What is not seen, because the focus was shifted and the movements are so subtle, is that in one smooth sequence of separate moves, the trainer slightly turned his head in each direction before ever so slightly shifting his center of gravity back and forth. Doing this also caused the trainer's leg opposite the direction the horse was asked to bend its neck to ever so lightly tense. It's a natural action of maintaining balance. It's also a classic example of "bait and switch." What a horse sees and feels is far more important than what it hears.

I have found one very practical and useful action that can be initiated by a sound, and that is for the horse to stop, plant all four feet, and stand still under any and all conditions whether I am mounted or on foot. Here again, uttering a sound exactly the same way every time is the key. The most common method for getting a horse to stop is the word "whoa." Of course, sometimes the person says "whoa," sometimes "whooooa," sometimes "ho," or "whoooa now," even "WHOA!" sometimes…okay, I think you get the idea. From the frequency of its use, I get the impression a lot of people must be operating under the assumption that "whoa" is part of a horse's DNA and that a horse is born knowing what it means because "whoa" is what is uttered whenever a horse presents any kind of emergency situation.

So what about this business of a horse learning to stop and stand still on an audible command? (Notice I said "audible" command, not a "word" command?) A number of years ago my wife, a very observant woman, told me she thought it seemed very unprofessional when people said "whoa" out loud in the show ring. A lot of the audience could hear it and even see it being said. Like most horse people, I'd never thought about that, but it made sense. So, I started saying "whoa" without opening my mouth. It kind of sounds like I'm just clearing my throat, and it is a totally unique sound. The advantage of this sound is that the horse can hear it just as easily as the spoken word, but no one else sees or hears it, and the only possible change in it is volume. It wasn't long before I found that my horse had learned to associate the sound with standing still, whether I was mounted or not. When I dismount I can simply show my horse the palm of my hand and say "hmmpt" (sound and sight together), and he is very good about standing in place until I either remount, use my reins or take-down-rope and lead him, or even just call him to me. This is the principle of a single given sound clearly meaning one, and only one, very simple thing and exactly the same thing every time. Reinforced with a visual command it is even more effective.

This brings us to a negative aspect of the use of sound. It seems to be natural for the human voice to get louder in relation to one's level of anxiety or excitement. To get a horse to respond, verbal commands are common. Should the animal get confused, nervous, or otherwise unresponsive, in attempting to establish stronger authority the command is often repeated louder. The louder the command is spoken the more confused and nervous the horse becomes until the horse finally just wants to run away. People are predators, and the horse knows it. In a case like this, the rider is attempting to communicate *to* the horse rather than *with* it, and the rider will get the exact opposite of what he wants. The horse interprets the sound as a predator's roar, so getting louder only serves to increase the horse's anxiety. This, in turn, produces even louder and more desperate "roaring" from the human predator pulling on the lead rope or on the reins, and the situation rapidly falls apart.

When a horse suddenly bolts and hits full speed in two or three jumps, more often than not a rider's natural reaction is to clamp his legs against the horse's ribs, yell "**WHOA**" at top of his lungs several times, frantically pull as hard as he can on both reins, all the while doing his best to maintain a death-grip on the saddle horn. In a situation like this everything a rider doesn't want to happen, happens.

Some detailed analysis reveals that there are many things involved when a horse bolts, and they all take place in the blink of an eye. A person has to learn to deal with this situation when it happens because the root cause will never be eliminated. For survival purposes, Mother Nature gave horses an adrenaline pump with a hair-trigger. Any unexpected loud sounds, quick movements, feather touch, or even some odors can set that pump off, and in a split instant a set of lightning-quick reflexes puts the horse in the escape mode which means only one thing – to run away as fast as possible and at all cost.

When a horse bolts, it begins with an unbelievably quick and very violent jump-start that puts every muscle and every nerve a horse has on a razor edge. This does a pretty fair job on the rider, too. This jump might be in any direction depending on the location of the frightening stimulus. This initial, violent jump often catches a rider, especially a novice rider, completely off-guard because a horse can see, hear, feel, and smell a lot of things to which an unsuspecting rider is oblivious. It takes a very experienced rider with years spent developing muscle memory and reflexes as quick as those of the horse to maintain his balance while simultaneously responding quickly enough to prevent this initial jump from escalating into a blind, panic runaway. By "quick enough" I mean a matter of a fraction of a second, usually less. This is not an exaggeration.

In the case of the novice rider, this initial jump nearly always comes as a complete surprise, and unless the rider has developed a very secure seat, he will immediately be thrown off balance from which he may not recover. Now, it is a fact that Mother Nature has also given humans quite a set of reflexes, but in this situation those reflexes work against them. In order to stay aboard (if he still is) the rider will, almost without exception, instantly and loudly yell "WHOA," and instinctively clamp his legs tightly against the horse to keep from falling off. A rider could not devise a better way to instantly put a horse into a fear-driven panic than the combination of these two things. Then, in quick succession and desperation, comes severe pulling and yanking straight back on the reins which causes the bit to inflict extreme pain. Everything a person does instinctively by natural reflex only serves to add fuel to the fire. In what is now a fear and pain induced panic, the horse forgets whatever it was that initially spooked it and instantly switches into attempting to either escape from, or get rid of, its rider. The horse does not have the ability to focus on two things at the same time, remember?

In the final analysis, the horse nearly always gets blamed for the entire episode because whatever spooked it was absolutely harmless – by human standards. Never mind that the rider instantly communicated to the horse, admittedly unintentionally, that there really was something to be afraid of and that it should make every effort to race out of there as fast as possible. Of course, in the horse's mind it made no difference whether the rider came along or not. In a survival situation it's everyone for himself. When the rider became scared and started yelling, screaming, kicking, and pulling, the horse's initial assessment of danger was simply reinforced, and it responded accordingly.

So, we can gather from this example that sound can be either one's best friend or worst enemy depending on when and how it is used or occurs. We can also ascertain that it is definitely in a person's best interests to practice and develop a set of reflexes that will work in his favor when situations like this arise. Notice I said "when" not "if," because if one is going to ride a horse I guarantee it's going to happen sooner or later.

When an experienced rider encounters this sort of thing, the rider will immediately, and without uttering a sound, usually pull the horse's head sharply around in either direction causing the horse to pour its energy into circling, thereby preventing it from bolting into an uncontrolled panic run. Also, a horse spinning in a tight circle can't buck very well, either, which means the horse will have a far more difficult time getting rid of its rider. Under these circumstances the horse shortly burns up all the adrenalin and calms down. Its focus will have been altered, control will have been maintained, and order will have been restored by adding as little excitement as possible.

There's an old cowboy saying that says, "When you find yourself in a hole, the first thing to do is quit diggin'."

What the heck was that strange noise?

(Photo courtesy of Barb Pritchard – aka Tumbleweed Tillie)

Notes

SIX

In the Eye of the Beholder

Take a good look at a horse's eyes. Especially notice how far apart the eyes are and that they are located on the sides of the horse's face. Then look very closely at the pupil of the eye and its geometric shape in normal daylight. These things are well worth noting because there are some very common issues related to eye placement and shape – issues that can have a tremendous impact on communicating with a horse.

In taking an objective approach to the eye, let's begin with what is commonly assumed about a horse's eyes. More to the point, what do most horse people *think* they know about a horse's eyes? The truth is, not much actual biological fact. Most people just unconsciously assume the horse sees what they see. If they see a piece of newspaper floating along the ground in a breeze, they assume that is what the horse sees. If they see something directly in front of them, they assume that's what the horse sees also. This could not be further from the truth.

Look at your eyes in a mirror. Your eyes are close together on the front of your face, and the pupils are round, right? Now look at a horse's eyes again. The pupils are about a quarter of an inch high, and about an inch long. Where are the horse's eyes located? On the sides of its face and about ten inches apart. Where are your eyes located? On the front of your face and about 2 ½ inches apart. So, with these obvious physical differences, wouldn't it make sense that a horse probably doesn't see things the same way a person does? The fact of the matter is, it doesn't. Not only does a horse not see things the same way a person sees them, but the horse doesn't interpret what it sees the same way a person does.

People have what is known as binocular vision. This means both eyes focus on the same thing at the same time. This is what allows humans to see objects in three dimensions and gives depth perception. In other words, a person can judge the exact shape and how close he is to an object. He can also tell how fast he is approaching an object, or how fast it is approaching him.

Horses are not that fortunate. They have what is called monocular vision. Each eye sees a different image. The left eye sees things on the left side of the horse, and the right eye sees things on the right side. Because each image is seen by only one eye, that image is not three dimensional. This means horses have extremely little depth perception. This is why they "spook" at things that move suddenly. At its extreme edge, human peripheral vision is also one dimensional. Vision isn't three dimensional until the object moves forward enough, or you turn your head enough, for both eyes to focus on it. This is why people tend to "spook" at things that move suddenly into their peripheral vision.

There is a long, narrow, v-shaped area in front of the horse where left and right views do overlap. This means objects in the distance are three dimensional, and objects that are close are not. However, because of the distance between the eyes there is also a v-shaped blind spot directly in front of the horse.

Mother Nature had a very good reason for equipping a horse in this manner. A horse's strictly vegetarian diet is primarily grasses, which don't generally have an extremely high concentration of nutritional value. So, to keep 1,000 pounds of muscle in good health, a horse must spend a lot of time grazing with its head down. Horses are also prey animals. Predators kill and eat them. With their eyes at the sides of their heads and the long narrow pupils that are parallel to the ground, horses have nearly a 360 degree view of their surroundings while they are grazing. This also means horses see two separate and distinct 180 degree images: one on the left and another on the right. A predator has a difficult time sneaking up on them. The equine brain allows the horse to focus on either both images at once or to concentrate on each image separately. If a horse sees anything move on one side of it, that side immediately becomes the primary focus. However, the other side is still active – it just isn't the primary focus, and it becomes very much like a human's peripheral vision. So, if a horse's attention happens to be focused on the left side and something suddenly appears or moves on the right side, the horse often startles. It makes no difference that the object or movement might be something with which the horse is completely familiar. The unexpected appearance of something when the horse's attention is somewhere else can still startle the animal and it will, as humans say, "spook." A horse may only "spook" for a split second until it recognizes the object, but if the rider "spooks" and takes immediate corrective action, the horse's attention is immediately shifted to the rider who is exhibiting a less than calm demeanor and probably pulling hard on the reins.

When a horse spooks as part of its survival mechanism, it receives an instant jolt of adrenaline. Couple this adrenaline rush with an excited rider's adrenaline rush trying to restrain the animal, and things can fall completely apart in short order. Just because the human didn't see any reason for the horse to either spook or fall apart doesn't mean the horse didn't.

A human eyeball is pretty much round. When the eye is looking at something close, like when reading this, the lens of the eye adjusts itself to the proper thickness for focusing the letters and words on the retina at the back of the eyeball. If you glance up to focus on something on the other side of the room, the lens will almost immediately change thickness so the image falling on the retina stays in focus. Consider a magnifying glass. If the glass is too close or too far away from an image, the image is blurred. This is why binocular lenses need to be adjusted for different objects at different distances. Moving the lenses closer together or farther apart changes the focus, much like the lens of your eye getting thicker or thinner.

The horse doesn't have the luxury of a lens that adjusts thickness to focus. Instead, it has an elliptical-shaped eyeball that is slightly longer from top to bottom than front to rear, and the lens is a fixed thickness. Therefore, to focus on something in the distance it must tip the eyeball to lengthen the distance between the lens and the retina. This is why when something in the distance gets a horse's attention, it elevates its head and moves its nose up or down to get a good focus. This is one of the reasons why horses that are running fast stick their noses almost straight out. They can focus way ahead on where they are going. To focus on something at its feet, a horse has to arch its neck, tuck its nose toward its chest, and tip its head to one side or the other to focus the image in only one eye. An object at its feet is too close for it to use both eyes since the eyes are so far apart. This is why a head position with the face perpendicular to the ground has been the mantra of good horsemen the world over for centuries. This position gives the horse a maximum 360 degree visual advantage.

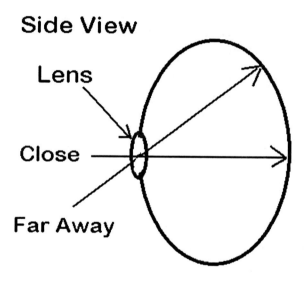

This also means the "cowboy" saying he wants his horse to "go with its head down so it can see where it's going" is pure nonsense. Now, it is a fact that the old-time cowboy actually did say this. However, it is also a fact that he was largely uneducated and inarticulate. He said "head" when he meant "nose." (In no Charles Russell or Fred Remington painting do you see a horse going with its head literally down.) With the head and neck literally down and the nose "tucked in" (*ala* today's western pleasure show ring) the horse cannot see anything ahead of it. The long, narrow pupil is more vertical than horizontal, so the horse sees more up and down than forward and backward. Only if the head and neck are elevated, the neck arched, and the face perpendicular to the ground does a horse have the greatest visual advantage. In this posture, the pupil remains parallel to the ground and the horse has a very clear picture of what is in front of it.

People tend to assume a horse sees, hears, and thinks the way they do, so there is also an unconscious assumption that it will respond to things the same way they would. Wrong again! Humans interpret and respond to the things around us in a manner unique to humans, and horses respond to the things around them in a manner unique to horses. It is a rare rider who truly understands this and learns to "think like his horse." Those who are able to do this invariably get labeled a "natural" or maybe even a "horse whisperer."

For thousands of years humans hunted horses for food. The animals that survived were those that developed the ability to instantly and accurately "read" the body language of their predators. Over the centuries this became so ingrained in the survivors that it became almost a part of their DNA and borders on the supernatural. Whatever a person's emotional state of mind, the person's horse will know it in a heartbeat. It is physically impossible to "fool" a horse by emotionally thinking one way and acting in another.

I'm sure you've watched TV or movie documentaries shot on the African plain where a pride of lions can be casually walking along very close to a herd of zebras. The zebras raise their heads and watch, but they don't panic and run. Why? Because the lion isn't hunting. A lion, or any predator for that matter, moves in a totally different manner if it is planning to kill its prey. The ability of the zebras to read the lion's body language tells them in a split-instant whether or not the lion is a threat. Zebras are not afraid of a lion simply because it is a lion. They are only afraid of a lion that wants to kill them.

A common complaint of deer hunters is that they see deer throughout the forest in the off-season but can hardly catch a glimpse of one during the hunt. Do they think the day before the season opens the deer can't hear, see, and smell a sudden overnight increase in the number of people sneaking around and a hundred out-of-the-ordinary odors in the air? Odors like gun oil, vehicle exhaust, campfires, cooking food, the pungent aroma of brewing coffee in the morning, human sweat, or even the perfume the laundry soap left in clothes when they were washed? Do they think the deer can't tell just by the way a person is moving whether or not he is a threat?

Sadly, our modern day, high-tech, electro-mechanical world seems to be hell-bent on doing everything it can to remove the need for people to understand the world of nature and how to deal with it. If you are going to have much to do with horses, you would do well to fully understand and accept the fact that horses have *not* lost that ability – at least not yet.

So how can the way in which a horse sees the world be used to a human advantage? The first thing to do is to give the horse credit for being able to see things humans very often do not. A person's whole field of vision, including peripheral vision, roughly covers the 180 degrees directly in front of him. Knowing a horse also sees what is behind it, a person would do well to be more aware of what is all around.

If you turn your head 90 degrees left, you will have about the same 180 degree field of view your horse has on its left except it doesn't need to turn its head. The same applies to the right. You will have the advantage of seeing it in three dimensions because you will be using both eyes. Your horse is only seeing it with one eye. Your horse has the advantage of being able to see you on its back without turning its head. If you are sitting straight, your center of gravity is in line with the horse's center of gravity.

The horse can also focus on its rider with either eye as it wishes. If the rider should lean ever-so-slightly to the left, his center of gravity moves left and the horse will focus on him in its left field of vision. Should the rider then wave his arm in the horse's right field of vision, the horse could easily startle since it was focused on the left field of vision. The field of vision in which the rider appears can give his horse a very clear "heads up" that it is going to be asked to perform some specific movement in the direction the rider has appeared and shifted his center of gravity toward. This allows the horse a split second to focus in that direction and become mentally prepared for a change of some sort. It doesn't take long for a horse to learn to simply move in whatever direction and manner will place its center of gravity back in alignment with its rider's center of gravity the second it sees the rider leave one field of vision and appear in the other. All the rider needs to do is be absolutely consistent.

This brings us to the subject of the physical touch....

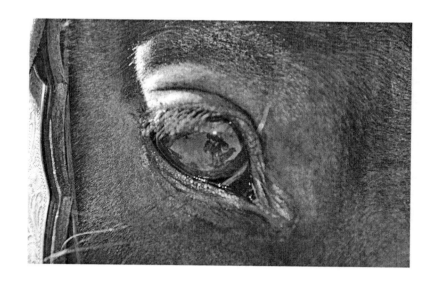

A close look here reveals the photographer, Barb Pritchard, reflected in Concho's eye

(Photo courtesy of Barbara Pritchard, aka Tumbleweed Tilly)

Notes

SEVEN

The Physical Touch

A "touch" is a physical action initiated by a perpetrator and felt by a recipient. "Feel" is how the recipient interprets a touch. Because there can't be one without the other, "touch" and "feel" are opposite sides of the same coin. Both of these terms need to be explored, because horse and rider are simultaneously both perpetrator and recipient of "touch."

What's the first image that comes to mind when you think about touching a horse? In all probability, the image is probably something along the lines of softly petting the horse's nose or stroking its neck. Hardly ever is the image one of taking hold of a horse's fetlock to pick up its foot, smacking it on the nose for trying to nip, or any of several similar actions where a person makes a conscious decision to make physical contact with a horse. Seldom considered is that the way people view these actions is often far different from the way the horse views them. What a person intends when they touch a horse doesn't mean anything to the animal. The horse will respond according to its own interpretation of anyone or anything touching it.

Human physical contact with a horse is seldom considered from the horse's point of view. For one thing, a horse doesn't differentiate between intentional and unintentional touches. For another, any physical contact with a horse is going to have some effect whether the person intends it to or not. Being the timid prey animal it is, a horse's survival instinct makes it acutely aware of anything touching it. It is critically important for a person to be aware of this because when physical contact is made, it is not at all unusual for horse and human to have different interpretations of the touch. Only if both horse and human interpret a touch similarly is the response of either going to be predictable.

Remember the previous chapter concerning a horse's field of vision? Should a horse be focused on something in front of it and its hindquarters are unexpectedly touched, a perfectly natural survival reflex is to spook or to kick.

Most people assume a horse will somehow automatically know what their touch is intended to mean, but it's not at all uncommon for a horse to interpret a person's touch far differently than a person intends. Remember the chapter on sound, where a very nervous person tries to sooth and calm a horse by crooning words the horse doesn't understand while stroking (touching) the equally nervous horse on the neck? Do you think the horse can't feel the tension in the hand stroking its neck? A horse can feel the tension in a rider's posture and in his legs. In these instances, "touch" and "feel" are both at work at the same time in both parties, just in two different directions. Neither party has any idea how their "touch" is affecting the way the other party feels.

How do you suppose you would react if a person, with totally innocent intent, approached you making sounds (talking in a foreign language) you didn't understand while attempting to stroke your face? What if, as you pulled away, the person got louder and tried to prevent you from pulling away while still trying to stroke your face? The fact that they were merely attempting to brush something of which you were totally unaware off your face wouldn't mean very much, would it? Of course not, and the situation would rapidly deteriorate into a physical confrontation, wouldn't it? The question is, which party, if any, should be shouldering the blame in this kind of a misunderstanding?

When a horse becomes startled or exhibits aggression toward a person, it isn't uncommon for the person to exclaim, "But I didn't do anything." Well, maybe the person didn't *intend* to do anything, and they may *think* they didn't do anything, but that wasn't the horse's interpretation. The interpretation of the "touchee" is always more important than the intent of the "toucher" in determining the outcome.

By a person simply sitting in a saddle he is touching the horse. Because there is a saddle between the horse and the rider there is an assumption that the horse is only being touched when the reins are pulled, a cue is given with the rider's legs, or the rider pats the horse on the neck. No saddle, English or Western, is going to mask what a horse feels with even the slightest move the rider makes.

Whether intentional or accidental, the most subtle movement of a rider can be felt by a horse just as surely as petting its nose, stroking its neck, kicking its ribs, or smacking it with a riding crop. The horse can both see and feel it when a rider even turns his head to look left or right, or up or down. These subtle moves rarely mean anything to a horse because most horses become totally use to them. But that doesn't mean that it *couldn't* mean something if applied with religious consistency and mild reinforcement.

If you've ever participated in ballroom dancing, you are familiar with communication by touch and feel. Each dancer is in constant physical contact with his or her partner with nothing more than their finger tips and the palms of their hands. The lady's right hand is held in the man's left hand. Her left hand is placed on his right shoulder, and his right hand rests on the left side of her waist. The lady takes her cues from the man. An imperceptible (to the viewer) increase in the pressure of either of the man's hands or fingers can instantly relay to his partner precisely what move to make, in what direction, and how quickly. The exact same "feel" can even mean a completely different type of move depending on where the dancers are in some routine they have learned through practice. If they've practiced enough and everything is timed right, nobody gets their feet stepped on or falls down.

Riding a horse is no different than ballroom dancing. Whether dancing or riding, if done correctly, no one watching can detect any signals, and the performance appears to be pure, flawless, spontaneous pleasure. With the rider leading, a horse can learn to immediately respond to even the slightest touch on the reins, pressure of a leg against its side, or any move that ever so slightly shifts the rider's center of gravity. So, for our purposes here "touch" and "feel" are going to be considered interchangeable terms.

Let's take a look at a very common occurrence. Anyone who's ridden much has noticed how a horse moves differently going away from the barn than going toward it. I'm not talking about the spoiled, barn-sour beast that runs uncontrollably back to the barn the way many a rental horse has done with a first time rider. No, I'm talking about the normal, everyday, run-of-the-mill, mild-mannered family riding horse. Almost without exception, when going in the direction of the barn the ride just feels different. The horse carries its head a little higher. Its ears are pointed forward more than usual, and the horse has more quickness in its step. No matter how well-behaved and well-mannered, how long the ride, or how tired the horse may be, it just seems to become a little more lively when heading home. This is quite common. It's no different with people. Horses really aren't all that fond of physical labor, especially if it isn't their idea in the first place, and they look forward with anticipation to returning to the barn, being unsaddled, having a cool drink, maybe enjoying a bath, being turned loose, taking a good roll, and working real hard at loafing for the rest of the day. If you are perfectly honest about it, that's not at all unlike the way you might get a little over-anxious when leaving work. You might try to "cheat the company clock" by a few minutes at quitting time. You chafe at the stop-and-go traffic because you just want to get home, take off your shoes, maybe take a hot shower, and kick back with a cold beverage after a hard day's work.

Where your horse is concerned, I'd almost bet there's something else about his trail behavior you've noticed and not been particularly happy with. That's when you are riding away from the barn (or in a direction other than the one your horse wants to go). You literally don't need to do any more than just turn your head in the direction the horse *does* want to go, and in a split-instant that's exactly where your horse is headed. This oftentimes catches a rider off-guard, and unless the rider is pretty quick the horse will gladly speed up to whatever it is allowed or thinks it can get away with. The reason this makes a lot of riders unhappy is because they know that getting away with this a few times can create an uncontrollable "barn sour" horse.

While this "barn sour" thing is most definitely an addressable issue, that's not what I want to talk about here. Instead, I want you to think about how simply turning your head can cause a horse's instant response to the direction you turned your head. The horse misinterpreted your move, but that's not the issue, either. The horse attached an immediate significance to something you considered insignificant. This is seldom considered but is very important. The very fact that a horse *can* be that sensitive to what its rider does in one situation proves it is capable of doing it in other situations. The *potential* is there. Now, whether or not a rider/trainer has the ability to tap into and utilize that potential is something else again, but it does prove it is possible. All (all?) that needs to be done is to figure out how to get the horse to understand what is expected of it at the slightest physical indication on the rider's part. Of course if the horse, like so many, has already spent years ignoring most of what its rider is doing because it seldom means anything, it is a little more difficult, but it can be done.

Just how does a person go about teaching a horse to pay close enough attention to its rider that it responds to a feather-light touch on the bit or an imperceptible shift of the rider's center of gravity? To train it to willingly cooperate with its rider, enjoy being ridden, and exhibit spirit and enthusiasm under saddle? Well, because it is easier (or I'm lazy, take your pick) I'm going to tell you how to go about *not* getting these things accomplished. To offend is not my intent.

To guarantee a totally insensitive and uncooperative horse, ride it for no more than an hour or two on the weekend, but only if it's convenient and you have nothing else to do. Then, while aboard the horse, slouch loosely *on* (not in – *on*) the saddle and flop around like a sack of potatoes. To absolutely guarantee failure, jab the horse in the ribs with a set of spurs every once in a while just to "keep 'im awake" and to remind him of your authority. Another very effective maneuver is to use a curb bit with a high center port and long shanks. Then pull real hard on the reins every few minutes just to keep his mouth "softened up." Roar out lots of orders to firmly establish your authority. Should the slightest disobedience be encountered, a good smack with a riding crop is a great way to pretty well mess things up. I will unequivocally guarantee this is a 100%, sure-fire method of producing a horse that will *not* respond to any pulling on the reins let alone a feather touch, will do *nothing* more than whatever you are able to physically force it do, will *not* enjoy being ridden, and *will* make every attempt to stay away from you as much as possible.

It just seems there is such a distinct lack of logic in the horse world. If whatever a person is doing is not producing the results the person wants, but they keep doing it, doesn't it stand to reason that the person is going to keep getting the same results? Wouldn't simple logic tell them they need to be doing something different?

Just for comparison, if someone is handling their horse in the manner outlined above, wouldn't it be logical to assume the exact opposite might very well produce the opposite results? Ride as often as possible, preferably every day even if it's only for a few minutes. Acquire a steady, balanced seat and a consistent posture in the saddle at all times. Help the horse remain as mentally relaxed as you can by not using spurs or a riding crop. Use a mild bit and stay off it as much as possible. Speak softly and calmly, if at all. Logically, I'd say this sure does sound like it could very likely be a pretty good start.

Go over those steps again and study them closely. It's not very hard to figure out that, practiced religiously, this routine would go a long way toward increasing the odds of eventually ending up with a horse that is a lot happier, more cooperative, and much quieter. Doing these things can quickly create an atmosphere that encourages the horse to respond to the slightest shift of weight in the saddle or touch on the reins. Not only that, but an unintended consequence of all this is that a person will probably become a much better rider.

The foundation of successful horsemanship is in acquiring a steady, balanced seat and a consistent posture in the saddle. The less a rider's body moves around when riding, the easier it is for the horse to take note of ("feel") when it changes. If a rider shifts his weight in a particular way, and then uses his reins and legs to encourage the horse to move in a particular way, the horse will begin to anticipate the rein and leg movements and will perform the desired move simply when the rider's weight shifts. Once it reaches that point, the weight shift can become less and less until it is almost imperceptible – imperceptible to anyone except the horse, that is.

The rider should move his body a bit like a joystick. When the rider shifts his weight in the direction he wants the horse to go, the rider's center of gravity moves in that direction. The horse can then more easily remain in balance and maneuver smoothly and more quickly by performing whatever move will keep its center of gravity in close alignment with the rider's. Sooner than one might think possible, a horse will learn to automatically move in whatever direction the rider's center of gravity shifts. Since the horse is making the decision to perform the move, the rider hardly needs to touch the reins except to maybe check forward movement. This is the absolute epitome of using the principle of touch and feel. Horse and rider are then a team and, like the ballroom dancers, will be able to put on a performance that appears to be pure, flawless, spontaneous pleasure, because that's pretty darned close to what it is.

Since a horse has trouble multi-tasking, there are advantages to the rider using his body like a joystick to indicate a change of speed or direction. The horse can be more relaxed because it isn't being blind-sided by an unexpected pull on the reins or kick in the ribs.

To achieve this level of expertise does not happen in sixty or ninety days. It takes a dedicated commitment and a large amount of time and effort on a person's part. It can take years. This is seldom possible in our modern, hectic, day-to-day schedules. However, don't let this discourage you and prevent you from trying, because whether you ever reach the highest levels as laid out here or not makes no difference. Any gains you make toward riding correctly and communicating in a manner your horse understands is going to result in you obtaining far more satisfaction out of whatever level you have the time and the patience to reach. You'll find yourself receiving a lot of pleasure out of every little gain, and the gains are cumulative.

What I've related here is not idle speculation. My horses and I can walk the talk and do so regularly for my living history audiences. I'm often asked to do a demonstration without a bridle or even a neck rope, and when I do so people will ask why I use what they consider to be a severe bit (a genuine Spanish spade) because it's obvious I certainly don't need one. Well, it's for the same reason you have power brakes and power steering on your vehicle – to get a high level of precision for the least amount of effort. Why do you carry a spare tire that you may never need? Because unforeseen and unpredictable situations over which you have no control have a nasty way of occurring, and it's very reassuring to have it…just in case. The same with a bridle.

Notes

EIGHT

Something Smells

I don't really know that the sense of smell can be considered a means of communication with a horse. It is, however, one of the ways a horse receives information, and smell can have a definite effect on a horse's actions, so it is well-worth looking into.

A horse's sense of smell is exceeded only by that of a dog's and, as I said earlier, not by much. If you've been around horses very much, you are aware that they tend to be a little more alert, or even a bit nervous, when a wind is blowing. The reason for this is that a wind will bring sounds and odors from a long way off. Even though the horse may be familiar with these sounds and smells, being unable to locate the source produces anxiety. Just like everything else, the manner in which a horse's handler reacts to this wind-caused nervousness can significantly add to the animal's nervousness or have a calming effect. It's no different than if you smelled something burning in your house but couldn't locate it. Imagine your reaction if someone who couldn't smell anything burning began physically chastising you for being nervous or scared. Do you really suppose this would have a calming effect on your state of mind? Of course it wouldn't. Well, it won't calm a nervous horse, either.

The harder the wind blows, the greater the distance away the source of the sounds and smells travels from. Even with no wind the horse can hear and smell things its handler cannot hear or smell, but the horse doesn't know this. A horse simply assumes its handler has the same audio and olfactory abilities it does, so it has every reason to believe its rider is upset and nervous for the very same reason it is. The horse can also smell the undetectable (to a human) odor of anxiety when its handler experiences nervousness or fear, regardless of how calm the rider may try to appear. If mishandled, this sort of situation escalates rapidly.

Most of us are familiar with the old adage that you don't want to let a horse (or a dog) know you are afraid of them. This has to be one of the worst pieces of bad advice a novice equestrian can be given. This advice has caused more than one person to be hurt, because it is impossible for anyone to hide his fear of a horse, from a horse. A person's posture, voice, and the manner in which he moves, coupled with the involuntary odor the body automatically gives off due to the adrenaline rush, will give the person away every time. The horse instantly detects that this predator (human) is afraid of it. The horse's survival instincts tell it to take full advantage of its situational superiority, and the horse will attempt to make the predator go away. This is a reflex-driven, survival instinct, and even in domesticated horses it is very much alive and well. As much as we would like to think differently, no amount of training can eliminate a natural, instinctive, reflex action. This applies to people as well as horses.

What is required when working with any horse is that you *actually not* be afraid. This is not to say there aren't horses and situations that require a heightened awareness, but this can be achieved without the fear factor. I'm well aware that overcoming fear is a lot easier said than done, but it *can* be done. If there is such a thing as a key element in the art of "horse whispering," it is a total lack of fear or anxiety in the "whisperer" when dealing with a horse.

There are several reasons a horse produces fear in people. The most obvious reason is the sheer size of the animal. The next reason a horse can inspire fear is that this half-ton of powerful muscle has a mind of its own. Then, to top it off, this huge, powerful animal can be as quick as lightning. Anyone can rapidly add all this together and conclude that the horse has the potential to be extremely dangerous. The first time a horse makes a move a person doesn't expect, even a non-aggressive move, a person's own survival instincts come into play and, thanks to adrenaline, the potential for danger becomes a reality.

So, how does a person go about losing his fear of the horse? The same way one goes about losing the fear of anything dangerous. Learn as much as possible about it. With an animal, learn how it moves and how it thinks. Learn what it likes and dislikes. Learn ways to let the horse know these same things about you. In short, learn how to communicate with the equine.

An important area of a horse's reaction to odor is one that is somewhat delicate and not necessarily easy to talk about. There are certain odors of reproductive origin that have a definite effect on a horse, and they are not all equine odors. The only thing predictable is that the results of these odors are often unpredictable.

Most horse people are aware that a stallion can be a real handful, especially around a mare. The natural urge to mate is one of the strongest urges known in the animal world. When a mare is in estrus (in heat, in season, etc.) the odor given off can send even a normally well-mannered stallion into a dangerous frenzy if restraint is attempted.

This is why a stallion should never be handled by anyone except those who have many years of experience doing so. This is also why, in most pre-20th century cultures, women were generally not allowed to handle stallions. For the same reason it was discouraged and often just flat forbidden then, it is still not a good idea, generally speaking. Historically, the reason for not allowing a woman to handle a stallion, which has a keen sense of smell, is because when a woman is having her menstrual cycle the odor can have a very strong effect on the way a stallion reacts to her. The stallion can become extremely aggressive. I'm pretty sure a 21st century woman's reproductive system doesn't function any differently than women's reproductive systems have always functioned.

Sometimes women, due to hormone fluctuations, can get downright testy. This can create problems between a woman and her horse (as well as between her and her man). A mare also experiences hormonal fluctuations. On many a trail ride, a horse that has approached too close behind a mare has been severely kicked.

Even the gentlest, most mild-mannered mare can become very aggressive if someone should attempt to handle her foal. The mare's natural instincts take over, and a person can quickly find himself in big trouble. When this happens the mare is very often punished, which teaches her a lesson.

Something seldom considered is that perfumes and colognes can trigger distrust in a horse. A horse is programmed to interpret the whole picture according to nature. How a person moves, sounds, and smells is supposed to relay the same message. If the way a person smells isn't synchronized with the way he or she looks and sounds, the horse may not be sure if it can trust the person. The odor of perfume and cologne can produce a state of confusion for a horse. Of course, this is more likely to apply to younger horses that haven't been around very many people or that don't know the handler. If it's an older horse that has been rented out for years and has been used to teach people to ride, or one the owner has been handling for years, this isn't going to be a big problem.

The issues just described are why a gelding (a neutered stallion) is generally preferred for riding, especially for a novice equestrian. The gelding tends to be more steady and reliable from day to day, year in and year out.

Speaking of geldings, it's a common assumption that if a stallion is an unmanageable hellion it will settle down if it is gelded. This doesn't work that way. What one will end up with is a male horse that is still an unmanageable hellion that can't reproduce. Unless a horse is gelded before it is sexually matured, roughly two years of age, there is little gain in this direction. If the horse has matured enough that the male reproductive hormones are embedded, the hormones will have permanently altered the horse's physiological makeup.

Although I've deviated from the sense of smell a bit, there is a thread of connection. All of these things play a very definite part in the way horses behave. How much you understand about the underlying reasons for horses behaving the way they do will have a major impact on how you act toward them. This, in turn, will have a major impact on how they act toward you.

Notes

NINE

Reward and Punishment

I'm not particularly comfortable with the mental image these two words normally produce in people's minds. Punishment is usually assumed to be the intentional application of some level of physical or mental stress, or maybe even pain. For most animals the reward is usually some sort of "treat" in the form of food. The theory is that the animal learns through what is basically fear and bribery. While this form of reward and punishment may work to a limited extent, it isn't the best way to go about establishing communication with a horse. (It doesn't work much better with people, either.) Reward and punishment, *if applied correctly*, are very much a part of equine communication, however, just not quite in the usually accepted form.

As a teenager I did a lot of riding with an excellent horseman who was many years my senior. Paul was a very quiet, patient man. I never saw him strike a horse, and seldom did I ever hear him even raise his voice to a horse. No matter how badly his horse might act up, he remained calm, quiet, and patient – calm almost to the point of *appearing* to completely ignore a horse when it would act up or openly rebel. Eventually the horse would finally settle down and Paul, without saying a word, would give it an affectionate pat on its neck and go on about his business as if nothing had happened.

One day I questioned his actions and Paul explained that he just didn't see any advantage in him adding any more excitement to the situation. He figured the horse was doing a pretty good job of that all by himself. Paul often said he thought working with horses (he never referred to it as training) was just too simple for the average person to understand. The more I work with horses the better I understand what he meant.

The priceless education I received from Paul was acquired in much the same way his horses received theirs. The education was never forced. I just very slowly and quietly absorbed it by being in his presence. One of Paul's many "bunkhouse philosophies" went something like this: "Discomfort makes a horse think; pain will cause it to fight." Being a teenager, even though I took this as gospel, the true significance of these words was beyond my limited understanding at the time. It was several years before I realized the absolute genius of them.

The effects of discomfort and pain are no less true for humans. We can get pretty ingenious and expend a lot of effort when it comes to our comfort. If we are cold, we devise a way to get warm. If we are too warm, we figure out a way to cool off. Given a choice, we will pick a chair (or a saddle) that feels good when we sit in it over one that doesn't. If that unreachable spot on our back itches, we find a way to scratch it. We are relentless in figuring out ways to consistently achieve comfort. Not only that, but once we do discover an effective method for eliminating some specific discomfort, we will immediately apply that exact same remedy every time that same discomfort occurs. On the other hand, should a situation be extremely painful, how much time, effort, and thought is spent figuring out, right then, how to prevent it from occurring again? Just like any other animal, our instinctive reflexes take over because clear thinking is reduced to zero when we experience pain. Pain, as an incentive to teach a horse something, seldom has positive results because it shuts down a horse's ability to react calmly. Instead, pain creates fear and anxiety, and that creates a survival driven fight or flight reaction. This reaction becomes more deeply imbedded with each recurrence. I fail to understand why this logic is so often ignored when it comes to communicating with a horse. This is not to say a rider or trainer can't use a horse's reaction to pain to achieve some immediate short-term goal. For the sake of safety it is sometimes necessary. However, this doesn't mean the horse has permanently learned anything – at least nothing positive.

Until a person accepts and fully understands a couple of key concepts, the odds of successful communication *with* a horse are not good. The first concept is that without physical comfort mental comfort is impossible, and without mental comfort learning is impossible. The second concept is that the equine brain is not sophisticated enough to grasp abstract concepts. Time, ownership, money, morals, status, and even simple right and wrong are abstract values unique to the human mind and often change according to circumstances. A horse will never intentionally do anything because of concern for an abstract concept. In a horse's mind it can do no wrong. It will react to any situation in whatever manner its equine brain determines is appropriate for its comfort and/or survival *under the circumstances at the time.* Nor will it ever give one millisecond of thought or concern for either the comfort or the safety of any human.

Once these basic concepts are fully accepted and understood, a person will find himself dealing with horses in a far different manner – a manner that tends to *prevent* uncooperative behavior and volatile situations instead of spending a lot of unproductive time dealing with rebellion. In other words, your efforts will become *proactive* rather than *reactive*, and you will find yourself preventing undesired results instead of dealing with them after the fact.

I doubt if most of you are much different than I in that you really don't mind doing an unpleasant task as long as it is your idea to do it. However, if told, "You will do it or else," there is a very strong tendency to say, "Oh, yeah! Watch and see." If you think your horse is any different, you are missing out on the opportunity to have the ultimate equine experience of having a horse willingly, and maybe even enthusiastically, do what you ask it to do, and do it for no other reason than that you asked and it felt mentally free enough to honor your request.

For an example of this marvel, let's do a little analysis of the one, single, most basic request every rider makes of a horse: to yield its nose to a pull on the reins and slow down or stop.

Unless it somehow learns differently, every animal on the face of the earth, including humans, will instinctively resist forcible restraint. This is an unarguable fact. If you think not, let someone silently come up behind you and, with no warning, suddenly wrap their arms tightly around your torso, pinning your arms to your sides. Most likely you would experience an instant jolt of fear, an adrenaline rush of biblical proportions, and your level of resistance would be proportionate to the force applied.

With this in mind, consider how most people assume a bridle bit is supposed to be used. The common assumption is that the level of control (or restraint) of a horse will be proportionate to the amount of force with which the reins are pulled. The harder the reins are pulled the quicker the horse will respond, right? After all, the harder you step on the brake pedal the faster your car will stop. The quicker you turn the steering wheel the quicker the car will turn. Enough force will slow down, turn, or stop anything moving, right? However, a horse is not an inanimate machine that responds predictably to applied force in accordance with the laws of physics. Horses will, like every other living creature, naturally and predictably resist applied force. They are living, responsive beings with a brain and a nervous system. They will never respond in the manner of a machine.

Calmly and quietly educating a horse on how it can achieve comfort is the key to working with a horse. Nowhere is this concept any more important or relevant than in applying a signal to the horse through the reins and bit. Unless you are pretty attentive you may have missed the subtle significance of the wording in that last sentence. It says, "applying a signal *to* the horse through the reins and bit," not "applying force *on* the bit with the reins." Let's talk about how the reins should be handled for maximum effect.

In the English disciplines there is often reference to developing "light" or "soft" hands. The manner in which the reins are held and applied is critical to communicating with a horse *through* the bit. At the risk of triggering the wrath of the "western" riding culture, the popular notion of "neck reining" is a myth. "Neck reining" is a crude technique "invented" by the American cowboys in the early 1800s as they watched the Mexican cowboys (vaqueros) work. The American boys were completely ignorant of the highly sophisticated, centuries-old, Spanish training methods that produced the finest cow horses the world has ever known. When the vaqueros were roping and herding cattle, they *appeared* to be guiding their cow horses by laying the rein opposite the direction of the turn against the horse's neck while holding both reins in only one hand. Because the movement was so subtle, the early cowboys never realized the Spanish horses were responding primarily to a slight shift of a rider's body, along with a small "tweak" of the direct rein with the lower three fingers of the hand holding the reins. This caused the horse to swing its nose in the direction of the turn, which then caused the rein on the outside of the turn to lay snug against the horse's neck while the inside rein went slack. This gave the appearance of a "neck rein." The cowboys, who were ignorant of formal equitation, never realized that in its early training the vaquero's horse was patiently taught, *through signals on the bit*, to keep its center of gravity aligned with the rider's center of gravity. When the rider leaned left the horse went left, or in any other direction so indicated by the rider. What looked like a "neck rein" to the earliest cowboys was nothing more than the result of the horse bending its neck into the turn, not the cause of the turn. Regardless, this misinterpretation has persisted, and it is proudly pointed to as one of the distinguishing features of the "western" riding culture.

These early cowboys were mostly uneducated, illiterate teenagers who had never been exposed to formal equitation of any kind. They looked down their cowboy noses at eastern "dudes," especially farmers, and had a lot of derogatory terms for farmers and how they lived. The cowboys called farmers names like sod-buster, squatter, nester, etc. There was no love lost for a farmer's way of life because the farmer's wire fences and crops threatened the cowboy way of life. Cowboys belittled and ridiculed anyone who handled a horse holding one rein in each hand. Holding the reins in two hands was considered the mark of a horse that wasn't as well-trained as their horses, or it was a sign of someone who was less of a horseman than they were. Since using both hands on the reins was the way farmers guided their work horses, cowboys called it "plow reining." To this day many less informed western riders still use the term and often with the same derogatory connotation. They consider plow reining to be far less sophisticated than neck reining, never realizing that when done correctly and carried to its highest level, it is the exact opposite.

If a "neck rein" is applied with force, the horse's nose is pulled in the opposite direction from the intended turn. With its neck *twisted* laterally and leading with the top of its head, the horse has no choice but to awkwardly navigate an out-of-balance turn. Conversely, a horse that responds to a rider's center of gravity *bends* its neck laterally into the turn, leads with its nose, and makes a smooth, balanced turn the same as if it were running free without a rider.

Then there is the argument that a person can't throw a lasso with both hands full of reins, so just how does a person riding with one hand go about properly sending a signal to the bit when a change of direction is desired? The fact is that without "soft" hands the odds are against one being able to do this.

Mount your horse in a fairly small enclosure. Either a round pen or square pen will do as long as it is big enough to allow the horse to move freely, but not so big as to allow it to run away. Position your elbows slightly in front of your hips with your hands just ahead of the front of the saddle about eight or ten inches apart and as low to the horse's withers as is practical. With the reins entering your hands from the bottom (or the little finger) take one rein in each hand holding it firmly between only the thumb and the forefinger. Your knuckles should assume about the same vertical angle as the horse's shoulder blades with the little finger farthest forward. The lower three fingers are *loosely* laid against the reins below the thumb and the forefinger. When a give-the-nose-to-the-left signal is to be given, first smoothly turn your head left and lean your upper body slightly to the left at the waist. This will significantly shift your center of gravity to the left. Doing this also automatically slightly increases the pressure of your right leg against the horse's side. Next, apply mild pressure to the left side of the bit with the left rein by slightly dropping the left hand and very lightly pushing the lower three fingers against the left rein. If there is no response, curl the lower three fingers of the left hand snugly around the rein. This will cause the horse to feel an increase in the pressure of the bit. If there is still no response, bend your wrist downward applying a bit more pressure. If there is still no response, without changing the position of the hand, move the left elbow rearward to just behind your hip about a foot or so and very quietly hold this position without varying the tension.

The horse is in an enclosure and can't really go anywhere, so just hold this position steady, leave the horse alone, and let it go wherever it wants. Even though turning the horse is your ultimate goal, at this point be less concerned with making the horse turn than trying to teach it something. The goal right now is to have the horse, on its own, figure out how to relieve the *discomfort* of the pressure on the bit. It may take a while the first time or two. The horse might go two or three rounds of the pen, but it will eventually get a little weary of being uncomfortable and it will then figure out how to get comfortable. At first it will probably try pulling against the rein, especially if that's what it has always done. The trick here is not to increase or decrease the tension on the rein. Hold it steady. Only if and when the horse, *of its own accord,* yields in the slightest to the tension do you release the rein. When the horse yields, releasing the rein must be done immediately no matter at which point in this entire process it happens. You want to impress upon the horse that it not only has control of the uncomfortable pressure on the bit, it can actually prevent it. If this process is rigidly and consistently followed, your horse will begin anticipating what part of the process is coming next and will start responding earlier and earlier in the process until eventually all you need to do is shift your center of gravity ever so slightly in the direction you want to go, and a feather touch on the rein (eventually just a wiggle) will send an imperceptible signal that calmly, quietly, and clearly communicates to your horse when to do what you want. Since the horse isn't being forced into anything, it will obey willingly. A level of communication will have been established by doing nothing more than giving the horse enough calm, quiet time to figure out for itself how to relieve the discomfort and learn full-well what you are asking of it.

The process just described is reward and punishment, not pain and pleasure. Eventually, the slightest shift in your center of gravity backed up with a feather touch on the rein becomes the "punishment" and the "reward" is the horse's total physical and mental comfort while willingly doing something you've asked.

Use this same technique when asking your horse to stop. Simultaneously handle both reins in the exact same manner as when asking for a turn. The only difference will be that you will shift your center of gravity ever so slightly rearward with a subtle "roll" of your hips while slightly increasing the pressure of both your legs against the horse's sides. (That's right, gently squeeze both legs.) You will be amazed at how quickly the horse learns to come to a well-balanced, collected stop because you are essentially asking the front of the horse to cease forward movement and at the same time "pushing" the hindquarters forward under the horse. In a shorter time than you might think, you will be able to stop your horse with little more than your hips and your legs ...... and at any speed.

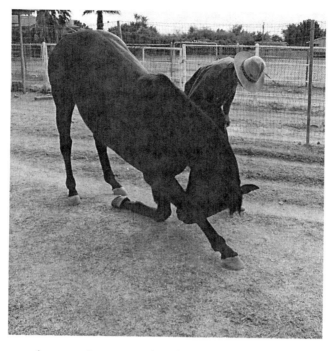

Appropriate equine rewards will help you attain your goals
(Photo by R.L. Coffield)

Notes

TEN

The Art of Timing

Quite a few years ago, as a young novice horseman, I was having a problem with a horse and asked a highly respected and very experienced trainer how to handle it. He said, "Well, when it feels about right, do this." He then, as is common with horse trainers, proceeded to demonstrate. I vividly remember thinking at the time, "Heck, I can do what he did, but how in %&@# am I supposed to know when it feels about right?" Regardless, his words were indelibly stamped in my memory, but it was several years before I fully realized just how right he'd been. What took so long to figure out what the trainer meant was that once I had enough experience and learned enough to know when it "feels about right," I didn't need anybody to tell me what to do. The man was talking about timing.

If anything can be pinpointed as the single most critical part of any physical activity it is timing, and there is no way to explain how to achieve it. Perfect timing is one of the things that sets the "horse whisperer" apart from the average horse person. The basic theory of working with horses is pretty much self-evident and not at all difficult to teach or understand. Timing, which is the art of learning the precise instant to perform actions, is the key to whether or not the desired results are achieved. Timing is also why these theoretically simple actions seem to work a lot better for some people than others. Perfect equine timing is an intangible, intricate, and complex mixture of the mental awareness, the physical sensitivity, the natural reflexes, and the developed muscle memory of *both* horse and rider. Should even one of these qualities be lacking in either horse or rider the results of the signals (cues) given to the horse will be some degree less than satisfactory.

Just consider what is involved when a person swings a bat at a baseball coming toward him eighty miles-per-hour. Both bat and ball are nearly the same diameter. There is the speed of the ball, the batter's reflexes, the batter's reaction time, the speed of the swing, and the batter's muscle memory. All these elements are part of determining precisely when the batter must start his swing and just where on the bat the ball has to make contact in order to go where the batter wants it to go. All these elements have to be simultaneously mentally processed and physically carried to completion within the split second between when the ball leaves the pitcher's hand and when it reaches the batter. Yet, as impossible as it sounds, people hit the ball. There are even people who can routinely and accurately determine whether to make the ball not only go high or low, but to left field, right field, or center field, and it's all a matter of timing. It wasn't learned from a book or overnight, either.

Timing is unique in that it can be learned but cannot be taught. If you think this isn't true, try to "teach" someone to ride a bicycle or roller skate using only lectures and books in classroom fashion. The best anyone can do is act as coach. Working with horses, or any animal for that matter, is a totally different situation. The bicycle and the roller skates are inanimate objects and unable to do anything of their own volition. An animal is a living, breathing entity with a functioning brain. It is capable of making its own decisions and carrying them out. Throw in the survival instinct and reflexes of both trainer and horse, and there is a serious potential for disaster. Considering the raw muscle power of a horse compared to a person, I can't think of one single reason for a horse to meekly yield to its rider's wishes under any conditions.

If timing is so critical and it can't be taught, just exactly how does a person go about learning it? That's an excellent question. Anything that is learned has to be taught by some means. In this case, timing is not taught, in its entirety, by another person or by reading a book. Both are very important sources of good information, but precise timing is only learned through many, many hours of studying and working with horses – hours of hands-on experience learning how and why horses move the way they do. It also involves a lot of trial and error. Horses will be the teachers.

Let's take a close look at what is actually involved in the simple, mechanical action of pulling the left rein asking a horse to turn left. The first thing that has to take place is for the rider to make the mental decision to go left. While this sounds simple enough it will, to some degree, involve each of the items in the above mentioned "complex mixture." The fundamental reason for making a left turn may or may not be completely arbitrary. Both horse and rider are capable of instigating such a turn. So, if a rider is approaching an obstacle and it makes no difference which direction he turns, he can leave it up to the horse to decide and the turn will be performed flawlessly. If it does make a difference, then the rider must make the decision. The outcome will be determined by the speed at which the horse is traveling as well as the reaction time, the reflexes, the physical coordination, and the developed muscle memory of both horse and rider. Precise timing of the signal to the horse involves not only an instant and *simultaneous* evaluation of all these things, the signal to turn must also occur at precisely the right moment in the horse's stride. This complex procedure is what equestrian timing is all about. The faster the horse is moving, the more important timing becomes. Regardless of how fast or slow the horse is traveling, if the timing is right the turn will be executed smoothly and will appear to be almost effortless for both horse and rider. If not, it is awkward at best and a total disaster at worst.

Should you doubt this, try walking a few steps in a circle to the right. Then, just as your right foot is leaving the ground, and without stopping, change directions to the left. Not real graceful, is it? This is because as the right foot is lifted the left leg is the only support, and you are leaning slightly to the right. To turn left with the right foot off the ground it must cross in front of the left foot, and the result is a very awkward and unbalanced change of direction. To smoothly transition to the left you need to step to the left as the left leg is lifted.

Try to imagine what would happen if you were running. It's considerably more graceful if the change in direction is done as your left foot leaves the ground. It isn't any different for a horse. Here again, reaction times and muscle memory are critical considerations. This left leg/right leg movement is absolutely critical when asking a horse for a change of leads.

Another good example of timing is the action of stopping a horse smoothly and quickly from a gallop. Now, I don't mean these ridiculous, spectacular, show stopping, half-the-length-of-of-the-arena, sliding stops. (I always thought the idea was to stop in as short a distance as possible, not see how far the horse could keep its balance in a controlled skid.) No, I'm referring to a smooth, quiet, and balanced stop in as short a distance as possible. A stop that's easy on both horse and rider. This is an impossible task unless it is performed in a fairly high state of collection. This means the horse must get its hindquarters well up under it as it puts on the brakes

There is a very real problem here. Imagine 1,000 pounds of horse in a very comfortable and relaxed long lope, and all this weight is being thrust forward at roughly twenty miles an hour. The horse has no idea that you intend for it to stop. The precise instant the signal to stop is given has a lot to do with the outcome. I think you can probably see where this is going: reflexes, reaction time, speed, coordination, muscle memory. However, even if all these things are under perfect control, if the signal to stop is not given when the horse is at precisely the right point in its stride the stop will still be awkward and physically hard on both horse and rider.

Let's look at the position of a horse's legs when it is galloping. Galloping, or cantering, is basically one forward leap after another. When a horse breaks into a gallop, it will rise up in the front and both front legs will be extended forward with the "lead" foot slightly ahead of the other one. The horse is then thrust forward by the powerful hind legs. As it "rolls" forward onto the front legs, the head and neck are extended forward to shift its weight forward and help both rear legs leave the ground. The rear legs are then brought forward under the belly with the same lead foot ahead of the other. As the hind legs are descending, the front legs are folding at the knees and coming up. For a split instant, all four legs are actually in the air at the same time.

As the hind legs hit the ground the front legs are again extended forward, and the entire sequence is repeated.

At what point in this sequence should the horse be given the signal to stop? It won't take a savvy rider long to figure out that it probably isn't a good idea to give the signal while all four feet are off the ground. Remember, the rider has to first make the conscious decision to stop. Then the rider's reaction time and physical coordination come into play in giving the signal. Once the signal is relayed to the horse, the horse's reaction time comes into play. All these things must be initiated and/or in place at specific points in the stride in order for the horse to come to a smooth, quick stop without stumbling and falling down. This timing can vary due to natural differences in the physical and mental abilities of horses and riders. Regardless, should any part of this sequence be out of time, the stop will not be smooth, and it can be hard on both horse and rider.

The point in the stride at which a galloping horse is given the signal to stop depends on the reaction times of both horse and rider. This is because to get stopped in balance the horse needs to initiate the stop when the hind legs are fully extended to the rear. At this point the horse is "rolling" forward over the front leg that isn't leading. The head and neck are extended forward and slightly down. Momentum is throwing the horse's weight forward to help both hind legs leave the ground. If the rider's signal has been timed correctly, the horse will, while the hind legs are coming forward, simultaneously lift its head and neck. This throws several hundred pounds rearward at the same time the hind legs are coming forward under its belly. In mid-stride the horse shifts nearly all its weight rearward to counteract its forward momentum, and the hind legs hit the ground and the horse assumes almost a sitting position and comes to a smooth, quick stop.

In other words, as the rear end goes down the front end comes up, and with the rider sitting on the pivot point of this action he hardly moves in the saddle. It's kind of like sitting at the center of a playground teeter-totter. As the horse plants its feet and quickly loses momentum, the rider is simply pushed down into the saddle seat rather than being ungracefully slammed forward against the fork.

If the timing is off and the horse receives the signal at almost any other point in the stride, especially with both front legs in the air, and it attempts to stop quickly, the laws of physics dictate that it will be an out of balance, stiff-legged stop with nearly all the horse's weight thrown forward onto stiff front legs. At best, the stop will be extremely hard on the horse's shoulders, back, and front legs. It isn't going to be easy on the rider, either. The horse will drop lower in the front which tilts its back at a forward angle in relation to the ground, and the rider is thrown hard straight forward. More than one rider has been thrown over the front of the saddle onto the horse's neck. This is almost a given if riding an English saddle, and very painful if riding a western rig with a saddle horn. If the rider is lucky, the horse won't stumble and do a forward somersault on top of him.

Fortunately, Mother Nature has seen to it that horses have a highly developed survival instinct, so they are very careful about not falling down and hurting themselves. These instincts make no allowance for the welfare of a rider. So, if the timing of a stop signal is off, more often than not a horse will simply slow down and dribble to a stop – if it pays any attention to the signal at all.

Timing has everything to do with whether or not a galloping horse changes leads when asked for a change of direction. When a horse changes leads in the rear but not the front it is usually because it was asked to change direction as it was rolling forward over the front legs and both hind legs were in the air. Timing is also why a loose horse seldom ever misses changing a lead. It is in complete control of the timing.

Timing is no less important when working with a horse from the ground. The only difference here is that the trainer needs to be in the right place as well. Where the trainer is in relation to the horse is very closely tied to the timing of the trainer's actions. If you recall, chapter five explained that a horse's field of vision has two separate, nearly 180 degrees of sideways vision: one for the left eye and one for the right. When working with a horse from the ground, the trainer is viewed with only one eye and not in three dimensions and with little, if any, depth perception.

Teaching a horse of any age to follow (or lead) properly is not a difficult matter. A person doesn't have to be around horses very long before discovering that standing in front of a horse and attempting to lead it by pulling on the lead rope will only get the opposite of what is wanted. Instead, place the horse at your right side, but between you and a wall or a fence. This will prevent the horse from turning its hindquarters away from you. When encouraging it to move, if you are in the front half of its left field of vision, it will tend to back up. Place yourself in the back half of its left field of vision, and it will tend to move forward. If you are at the exact center, it will tend to either stand still or move in whichever direction it thinks will be to its advantage. Therefore, to get the horse to move forward from a standing position, shift your image slightly behind the center of the horse's left field of vision. Timed right, you and the horse will then ideally move forward at the same pace. The further you are to the rear of that field of vision the faster the horse will tend to move away. Too far rearward and the horse will bolt forward and turn its hindquarters away from you in a half circle and face you when it reaches the end of the lead rope. If too far in the front half of its field of vision, it will stop and quickly back up. You usually lose the resulting tug of war. There is a very delicate balance point in this business of positioning yourself in the horse's field of vision, and you will need to make very definite, but not necessarily quick, moves back and forth a few times at first to achieve the desired end result.

To stop the horse, step into the forward half of its field of vision and slightly toward the horse. The wall or fence on its right will prevent it from turning away and it will stop. If you are consistently in the right position at the right time, any horse will quickly learn to walk beside you on a loose lead rope with its head slightly in front of your shoulder. It will move forward when you move forward, stop when you stop, and even back up when you do. Done right, it will even turn left and right when you do without the lead rope ever getting tight.

When first teaching a horse to work on a long (or lunge) line, where you stand in relation to the horse's field of vision is critical. When facing the left side of the horse and you want it to move off to the left, you must place yourself slightly to the right of center of the horse's left field of vision. To the horse's way of thinking, this puts you behind it and it will tend to move forward. Once the horse is moving in a circle to the left and you want it to stop, you only need to take an obvious (to the horse) step to the left, putting yourself in the front of center of the horse's left field of vision. To the horse's way of thinking this puts you in front of it. Should the horse stop suddenly and turn toward you, a quick step or two to the right at *precisely the right time* will keep you in the rear of the horse's left field of vision and it will either stop or move off to the left again. The timing of these back and forth, left to right steps will have a far more positive effect than cracking a whip, loudly yelling "whoa," or any amount of pulling on the line. Eventually, the slightest shift of your body to your right or left foot will be perceived by the horse and it will respond accordingly. Again, there is a very delicate balance point, and the more consistently you work, the finer this point becomes.

Whether on the ground or on its back, working with a horse is no different than a couple performing a ballroom dance. Only one person can lead. If the person leading doesn't give the signals at just the right time, has a poor sense of rhythm, or isn't in the right place, it can quickly get awkward. When dancing, the pace of the music determines the rhythm. When riding, it's the gait and pace of the horse that determines the rhythm. Because a horse has a top heavy, horizontal shape and has to manipulate four stilt-like legs, it is mandatory that it perform every move with a rhythm. That's the only way it can keep from getting all those legs tangled, maintain balance, and stay upright.

Fortunately, with proper communication a horse is more than willing to allow us to lead in the art of dancing with them which, in every sense of the word, describes exactly what we are doing. Unfortunately, for various reasons not everyone has the physical coordination required to perfectly synchronize the timing of their signals to the horse with the rhythm of the horse. This doesn't mean only those gifted by nature with a high level of sensitivity and coordination can successfully ride a horse. It merely means that some people are going to be better at it than others. Those who are less gifted can still achieve a very acceptable level of horsemanship through diligent study and practice. The highest levels of horsemanship are unbelievably delicate and intricate combinations of both mental and physical skills that do not always come naturally, are not learned easily or quickly, and are just as true for the horse as the rider.

Like most everything else where horses are concerned, the honing of one's timing skills isn't difficult. What it takes is a dedicated combination of study and practice along with generous allowances made for a learning curve on the part of both horse and rider. Don't be too hard on yourself or your horse when things don't go as planned. It must also be recognized that horses have every bit as much variation in their physical and mental capabilities as people. These variations are the primary reason why some horse and rider teams seem to be more coordinated, move more gracefully, and appear to do what they do with so little effort on the part of either horse or rider. It is a rare and beautiful thing when the capabilities of horse and rider are perfectly matched. Intimate knowledge coupled with perfect timing is the intangible reason only a very few ever achieve the magical and mystical level of the fabled "Horse Whisperer."

Notes

ELEVEN

Muscle Memory

The subject of muscle memory is rarely brought up in the horse world, but without muscle memory the highest levels of communication with a horse cannot be achieved. For example, should you visit France but not speak the French language, learning a few key phrases and carrying a French-English dictionary around will probably help you. However, to achieve the most effective communication you must learn to speak French as fluently as you speak your native language.

After learning the equine language, developing muscle memory is the next most critical aspect of good horsemanship. Muscle memory is also probably the most overlooked aspect of good horsemanship, if it is even recognized at all. Since the vast majority of communication (signals, cues) with a horse is physical, the development of muscle memory is the glue that will bond horse and rider to the point where the two are able to think and respond as a single unit.

We are not born with the ability to walk upright balanced on two legs. It takes years during our early childhood to develop a very complex set of muscles and permanently hard-wire each of the delicate movements to our subconscious memory. Once the ability is developed, a person can walk, run, jump, and perform an amazing number of physical gyrations without a single conscious thought as to how it is done.

If a person intends to become a proficient horseman, he or she would do well to understand muscle memory because it will be necessary to develop an entirely new set. As with most athletic efforts, and riding a horse is most definitely an athletic effort, the older a person is before attempting the feat the more difficult it is to develop muscle memory and the longer it takes. In other words, this means patience and tolerance for error are mandatory.

Just what makes this muscle memory development so important? Whether you are aware of it or not, if you've ever attempted to ride a bicycle you understand its importance. It is almost impossible to describe precisely when and how much to simultaneously adjust the position of the handlebars and shift one's body weight to keep a bicycle upright. How does a person know precisely how far to lean into a corner in order to maintain that critical balance? Anyone who has ever become even a fairly good roller skater or skier understands muscle memory. It's what allows a person, with no conscious thought whatsoever, to keep the side with the wheels on the skates next to the ground, or the bottom of the skis next to the snow.

In any physical activity, timing and balance are critical factors. A successful performance depends on the delicate activation of hundreds, if not thousands, of very specific muscles that have to function faster than the brain can tell them to function. This makes the development of muscle memory absolutely mandatory. In no activity is this any more critical than horsemanship. It begins with the posture required to simply stay astride a moving horse which is nothing like sitting on a chair, which is precisely where the novice invariably makes his first mistake.

Every normal move a horse makes is made with a natural rhythm. Until a rider has spent enough time on a horse's back to program every muscle in his body to automatically respond in synchronization with the natural rhythmic moves a horse makes, he cannot become a truly accomplished rider.

Please, do not misinterpret this to mean a person cannot enjoy riding a horse until this happens. You don't need to be able to compete in the Indianapolis 500 race before you can enjoy taking your automobile for a Sunday afternoon cruise. Neither do you need to be NFL material to thoroughly enjoy a darned good game of backyard football at a family picnic. There are many, many levels of horsemanship. What I'm referring to is the level of skill required to successfully reach the horse world's equivalent of the Indy 500 or an NFL game, a level at which horse and rider think, react, and move as a single unit - the Fred Astaire/Ginger Rogers team of the horse world, if you will.

The level of horsemanship a person achieves depends on three things: how well he can communicate with the horse, his level of developed muscle memory and, in no small measure, the person's degree of natural physical abilities. It's a hard, cruel fact of life that some of us are born with more physical coordination than others. This is no less true for horses. Horses have varying degrees of physical and mental abilities and can quite often have a lot of one or the other, but not both. To find one with a high level of intelligence along with perfect conformation and athletic ability is rare – horse or human. In essence, however, this does seem to be the goal everyone strives to achieve. We all know absolute perfection is simply not possible, but that is still the challenge nonetheless, isn't it?

Three types of physical response come into play when riding a horse: reflexes, habits, and muscle memory. They apply equally to both horse and rider. A reflex is "hard-wired" into the nervous system at birth. Things like breathing or blinking the eyes are reflexes. Habits are routines learned by doing something often and consciously. Activities such as fastening a seatbelt before starting an automobile become habit if repeated often enough. Muscle memory differs from reflex and habit in that it is a learned response to a specific stimulus that eventually becomes "hard-wired" into the nervous system much like a natural reflex. Muscle memory is an immediate, unconscious, and correct automatic muscular response to the demands of a specific physical stimulus or circumstance, even if that stimulus or circumstance is not anticipated. The response can be so quick, smooth, and automatic the person (or the horse) may not even be aware it took place.

If this isn't quite clear, before you read any further simply stand up and walk across the room then come back and sit down. Go on. Do it. I'll be here when you get back.

Now, try and explain, move by move and in every minute detail, exactly how you did it. Then consider how much conscious thought was required on your part. Keep in mind, now, there were no reflexes involved. You were not born with the ability to walk upright. What took place was a conscious decision to perform an unbelievably complex physical action, but no conscious thought whatsoever was required as far as how to accomplish it.

This is the essence of muscle memory. The process of developing muscle memory requires that a muscular response be performed identically over and over and over until the nervous system is programmed to automatically trigger that same muscular response whenever the same stimulus is encountered. Once this programming is solidly in place the nervous system actually bypasses the brain and the programmed action is performed with almost no reaction time and with no conscious mental effort on the part of the person. This means that not only must the exact same action be performed repeatedly, it must be performed in response to exactly the same stimulus repeatedly.

Because of the way humans (and horses for that matter) are made, any new or unfamiliar physical action tends to be pretty clumsy at first. The more often the action is repeated in exactly the same manner the smoother it gets, which enables it to be performed faster until it eventually becomes permanently programmed into the nervous system.

Riding a bicycle is a good example of a conscious decision to perform an action that is impossible without muscle memory. This process doesn't happen overnight and the only way to hurry it up is to practice with rigid consistency and frequency. However, once the ability to ride a bike develops, you never have to learn it again. It may lose some of its sharp edge through lack of use, but muscle memory is permanent and that sharp edge is easily regained.

I've watched many good riders and trainers. Every good, accomplished horseman I've ever seen does things that I'm convinced they aren't even aware they are doing, and nearly all of them involve muscle memory. For example, any good horseman will tell you how important it is for a horse to bend its neck and "give you its head." With no argument, he is absolutely 100% correct. This is an unarguable fact that horsemen have known for over 3,000 years. But, let's take a real close look at what takes place when a rider demonstrates what it should look like when done correctly.

For our purposes here, let's say the trainer will have the horse yield its nose and "bend" to the left. What nearly everyone sees is the trainer giving a light pull or maybe just a tap on the left rein and, with no resistance whatsoever, the horse stands perfectly still and turns its head quietly and smoothly about 90 degrees or more to the left and stays in that position without restraint. So, since bending a horse's neck is proven gospel, you go home determined to teach it to your horse. You tug on the left rein and get hard resistance from a very stiff neck. So you pull progressively harder and harder until the neck bends a little. However, the neck will remain "bent" only so long as you keep steady pressure on the rein. Your horse's neck responds like a big spring. So, how did that trainer accomplish what he did? Well, for one thing, it didn't happen on the first try…or the second…or maybe not even on the twentieth. It was the result of an accumulation of many hours of repetition over a long period of time…maybe months. Even then, whether the trainer was aware of it or not, he did not just simply tug on the rein.

Had you watched the trainer very closely (not the horse, the *trainer*) as he performed this maneuver you would have seen him first turn his head ever so slightly to the left and possibly even tilt the chin downward. Simultaneously, he ever so slightly shifted his upper body to the left as he dropped his hand downward and the rein made contact with the bit. These four distinct actions would have smoothly taken place in a matter of milliseconds before the horse felt any movement of the bit in its mouth, if it even did at all. Those actions – looking left, shifting left, dropping the hand, left rein contact – always smoothly took place in the exact same sequence with little, if any, pause between them. At first each move, or step, would be a somewhat exaggerated, deliberate, slow, and completely separate action but still done with a smooth transition from one to the next. In addition, the trainer's right leg also had to tense, ever so slightly, simply to help him keep his balance. As the horse became more familiar with the sequence, the sequence was slowly speeded up until the actions came so close together and were executed so smoothly they gave the appearance of being one single action. Each of these moves (steps, signals, cues) became less and less pronounced to the point of being totally unnoticeable, especially to a novice viewer.

Whether or not the trainer, who has performed this sequence thousands of times, is fully aware of what all he is doing, you can bet the horse is aware. Then, when contact is made with the horse's mouth through the bit and its head quietly comes around to the left, the trainer, with profound authority, says something to the effect, "It is very important that you be able to have your horse quietly bend its neck and give you its head in this relaxed manner." Of course the only thing most people saw was the light tap on the left rein. They were totally unaware of everything the trainer left out of the explanation and demonstration.

In reality, the horse was very quickly anticipating what the trainer was going to do next. The slightest shift of a rider's center of gravity can very clearly communicate to a horse what it is going to be asked to do, and only a touch on the rein is needed to tell it when. Once that is accomplished it is repeated over and over until the response is hard-wired into the horse's brain as muscle memory. It only *appears* that all the rider did was tug a little on the rein.

Another item entering into the equation that was discussed earlier is that a horse's eyes are located at the sides of its face with an oblong pupil that is parallel to the ground. A horse's nearly 360-degree field of vision allows it to see to the rear as well as to the front. The instant the trainer turned his head slightly to the left the horse, due to the trainer's consistency, had a "heads-up" on what might be coming next. If the rider is consistent enough, the horse soon learns that once the trainer looks left there is likely to be, in quick succession, a slight leaning to the left, a dropping of the hand, and a tightening of the muscles in the rider's right leg followed by a light tap on the side of the bit to which the trainer shifted. By doing this with rigid consistency the trainer is developing muscle memory in the horse, and it will eventually respond to the rider's shifted center of gravity with no hesitation whatsoever on the horse's part.

Many people who seem to "have a way with a horse" are accused of not wanting to share their "secrets" when the truth is that they have always just simply done what they do without ever really studying their procedures in depth. They can't tell you what they do because they honestly are not aware of what all they are doing. They only know that whatever they are doing works. However, should their "expert opinion" be asked they sort of feel pressured into saying something more intelligent than, "Gee, I don't know, I just do it." What often happens in a case like this is that an incomplete and often very misleading explanation is given.

But, suppose the rider is simply looking to the left and doesn't want the horse to turn his head left. Good point. When a person anticipates making even the slightest physical movement an unbelievable number of subtle, involuntary things take place of which the person is not necessarily aware. Are you aware of all the hundreds (maybe thousands) of delicate muscle contractions that have to take place to simply prepare you to stand up from a sitting position? No, of course not, but that doesn't mean they don't take place, does it? They also take place a few milliseconds before you actually initiate the action. So, the moment a rider makes a mental decision to turn a horse to the left, the rider's whole being automatically and unconsciously prepares itself for the coming move. The rider's entire muscular structure changes ever so slightly as he unconsciously shifts his center of gravity to the left in anticipation of the coming turn. If the rider is simply looking to the left, none of this preparation takes place. If you think these delicate differences that are imperceptible to a viewer and often oblivious to even the rider can't be felt by the horse, you are badly mistaken.

A graphic example of these perfectly natural actions occurs when you are driving an automobile. If you turn to simply look out the left window you remain sitting straight up. If you anticipate making a left turn, you will not only look to the left, you will ever so slightly lean to the left in proportion to the speed of the vehicle and how tight you anticipate the turn will be. The lean, or shift in your center of gravity, is also invariably a split second before you begin to make the actual turn. This is nothing more than the perfectly natural action of maintaining one's balance.

You may now wonder why when you lean left the horse doesn't turn left. You must remember that when you are riding a horse there are two living, breathing, responsive, and feeling creatures involved, and if push comes to shove, each is far more concerned with their own welfare and safety than anything else. If you will recall I said earlier that, "Until you have spent enough time on a horse's back to program every muscle in your body to respond automatically to all the natural rhythmic moves a horse makes, you cannot become a truly accomplished horseman." Until this is accomplished you are probably not going to be steady, comfortable, and relaxed on the back of a moving horse under nearly all normal conditions. When people are not comfortable in a situation, they cannot fully relax because mental anxieties won't allow it. Mother Nature has programmed the human body to respond in a specific and predictable manner to mental anxiety. A general tenseness takes place, a little sweating may occur (remember that unbelievably acute sense of smell a horse has?) and due to the ever so slight tension in your whole body, any movement on your part tends to be a little bit jerky and maybe even a little erratic. A horse easily detects this which, in turn, tends to cause a certain level of anxiety in the horse. This causes the horse to move and respond in a less than relaxed manner because it figures that there must be something to be anxious about because of the way you are acting, but the horse can't see, hear, or smell what it might be. You then sense the anxiety in your horse and maintain your anxiety. If this occurs often enough the situation is eventually accepted by the horse as normal when you are aboard.

Without a well-tuned system of muscle memory that will let you relax under stress, you will not have the confidence required to concentrate on giving your horse confidence in you. Even if the horse eventually accepts your tenseness as normal, without the required muscle memory you will have to consciously try to keep yourself in a balanced position. On a horse this invariably translates into a fairly stiff vertical posture with both legs gripping the horse's sides to some degree in an attempt to maintain a steady seat. If the horse acts up even a little bit this posture is, of course, impossible to rigidly maintain at all times or for any length of time. Therefore, even though you are able to stay on its back you will be completely out of sync with the horse and, from the horse's point of view at least, pretty much all over its back most of the time. The horse may not have any idea whether you are leaning left because you want to make a turn, or if you are simply attempting to stay aboard. It's getting a lot of mixed and inconsistent signals and eventually pays little attention to most of them unless they are applied with enough force to become obvious to the animal.

Before a rider can physically communicate with his horse and not have the animal either ignore it or interpret it as an act of aggression, he must first develop the necessary muscle memory to ride in a steady, consistent, confident, and relaxed manner under any normal circumstance as well as a lot of unexpected ones.

As mentioned earlier, when I was a teenager I had the good fortune to spend a lot of time riding with an elderly gentleman who was a first rate horseman. He couldn't read or write, was old enough to be my grandfather, and passed on many years ago. However, horses were a common interest and we enjoyed each other's company. As a young man he had "cowboyed" all down through the American Southwest in the early 1900s when it was real wild-and-woolly cowboy country. At well over seventy years of age he was still starting two and three-year-old horses under saddle and could put a "handle" on a horse that made the hair at the back of your neck tingle and bring tears to your eyes when you watched it perform. I never saw him strike a horse, jerk a rein, or leave a spur mark on one. Seldom did he ever even raise his voice to a horse. His bunkhouse philosophies were, as he put it, "probably too simple for the average person to understand." I admired the man and his abilities and took his philosophies seriously. They've served me well for over half a century. Here are a few examples:

1. Just forget the mistakes and praise the successes. The horse doesn't know what it did was a mistake.

2. If your horse can't do it slow, no way in hell is it going to do it fast.

3. Any damned fool can make a horse run...that takes no talent whatsoever. It does, however, take quite a horseman to get a horse to walk when it wants to run.

4. The biggest secret to ridin' a horse is to just sit there like you was sittin' in church when he's comin' all apart underneath you.

Paul was also the only man I ever knew who could roll a smoke one-handed while riding a horse. That hasn't got anything to do with what we're talking about here, but it is kind of neat, isn't it? Anyway, take a good look again at that number 4 above. He was essentially talking about a rider's muscle memory. Until you can just calmly sit there until the horse settles down you will do nothing except add fuel to the fire. If the horse starts coming apart and you do also, no matter how it turns out, the end result is not going to be a positive one.

So, for the sake of moving on with this muscle memory topic, from now on let's assume you have spent the required amount of time in the saddle to just sit there in calm synchronization with your horse under almost any normal riding circumstance and even a few abnormal ones. Your muscle memory is unconsciously on duty every second you are aboard and will not allow you to be caught off-guard. We're also going to assume you are able to effectively communicate with your horse.

You are now in a position to do some serious horse training – the kind of training that will start rumors of "horse whispering" and all sorts of other equally ridiculous comments. You have absolutely no anxiety or conscious thought on your part about "keeping one leg on each side and your mind in the middle." Your fine-tuned riding abilities will now give you the mental freedom required to fully concentrate on adjusting your horse's behavior with few concerns about your ability to stay in the saddle.

Not until you reach this level of riding skill can you even begin to effectively develop the muscle memory required in the horse itself. You see, developing muscle memory in the horse is what horse training is really all about. No one in the entire history of horse\human relationships has ever taught a horse *how* to do anything. By their very nature horses are able to perform every action we require. All we need to do is figure out a way to get them to do these things only when we ask for them. In other words, horse training is nothing more than somehow letting a horse know *when* to do something it naturally knows how to do anyway. This is normally done by the rider giving the horse some signal or cue. Only when this cue is applied in exactly the same way every time, means the same thing every time, and the horse responds in exactly the same way every time is muscle memory being built in the horse. In the horse, just as in the human, it has to be learned slowly and in systematic increments. Then it is just as systematically and incrementally slowly transformed into muscle memory.

There is one other thing that has nothing to do with communicating or muscle memory, but anyone who intends to ride horses had best get it through his or her head right off: it isn't a matter of *if* you go off of a horse - it's a matter of *when*. If, for any reason, you find this unacceptable, then I would suggest you not get on one in the first place.

113

Before I was ten-years-old I'd lost count of how many times some horse had very ungracefully re-acquainted me with mother earth. As I stated in the introduction to this book, when anyone tells me they've never been "thrown off (or fallen off) a horse," I can be pretty certain one of only two things is true:

1.   They haven't ridden enough yet, or...
2.   They're not telling the truth.

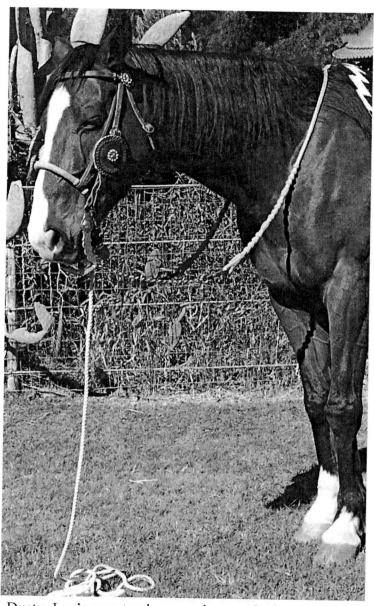

Dusty, Lee's race track rescue horse relaxing *his* muscles!

Notes

TWELVE

What Nobody Talks About

Be they good, bad, or indifferent, every horse trainer who has ever existed has been guilty of doing something that isn't dared to be talked about in today's world: equine punishment. It's not that punishment is anything that isn't necessary. It is, in fact, unequivocally absolutely critical to producing safe, manageable, well-mannered, and trustworthy horses. It is especially critical should the horse ever, for any reason, happen be ridden, handled, or come under the care of a novice.

Why is this subject such a taboo? There are three very good reasons. First, and most importantly, if punishment isn't done correctly, the horse will sooner or later hurt someone. The injury may only be a minor bruise, or it could be a fatality depending entirely on circumstance and luck. Second, as critically necessary as it is, there are misguided souls who will, with admittedly nothing but the purest of honest and good intentions but little knowledge of the natural world, blow equine punishment all out of proportion and hold those doing it legally liable in today's "sue-happy" climate. Third, punishment will inevitably be misinterpreted and misused by inexperienced novices. Misuse can cause irreparable mental damage to a horse, possibly physical damage to a handler or rider, and totally destroy the reputation of those openly admitting to doing it. It is a subject one will be hard pressed to read very much about in any horse training manual or hear publicly advocated by any professional horse trainer because it is so easily misconstrued, misunderstood, and misused. With all my previous expounding on how to communicate with a horse and being extremely careful not to create an atmosphere of fear, I'd like to do what may appear to be a little back-pedaling and address the topic of physical punishment.

If a person spends enough time around horses, there will inevitably be limited instances when, for the sake of long-term and many times immediate safety, very definite aggressive physical action must be swiftly and firmly taken against a horse.

You seldom see a horse physically disciplined in public for the same reason you don't see a child physically disciplined in public in today's world. A person would be turned in for cruelty by someone who means well enough but hasn't a clue as to what is really going on. It makes little difference to the uneducated that the only effective time to punish is immediately upon, and in proportion to, the deserving offense. And if we are perfectly honest, we've nearly all observed both children and horses that most certainly did deserve some form of punishment.

The real problems start the instant a child or a horse comes to the realization that there are circumstances in which there are no significant consequences for whatever they are doing. As desirable as it might be to live in a perfect, non-violent, Pollyanna-style world where everything is soft and fuzzy and gentle, and every living creature is nice to every other living creature, the reality is that when a horse discovers it can push people around things can get extremely dangerous in short order. A horse has no conscience and could care less should it purposefully or accidentally hurt or even kill you. History is full of people who have been severely injured or died as a result of being bitten, kicked, or thrown by an ill-mannered, aggressive horse. The crushing power of a horse's jaws can snap any bone in the human body like a toothpick.

Since I have no public profile to protect and am not relying on building one to make a living, I have nothing to lose by stating the truth in this matter. Please understand, I most assuredly neither advocate nor condone any cruel measures, and I will not tolerate animal abuse in any form. Anyone who knows me and my horses will attest to this fact. I do, however, advocate a very firm hand in physically establishing a human's authority over a horse at the slightest indication of potentially dangerous aggression by a horse.

In any group of two or more horses there is, by nature, a definite pecking order, and there is hell to pay should a horse violate its place in that order. If you are fortunate enough that your horse has allowed you into its world, you will have to "play the game" by its rules and establish in its mind that you are a notch or two above it in the pecking order. If you don't, I can assure you that your horse will establish himself a notch or two above you. It is a part of a horse's natural makeup, and horses are big, powerful, and quick. That is a dangerous combination in an animal that acts toward you as if you are beneath it in the pecking order.

Very early in a relationship with a human, a horse will test its trainer/rider. This is a perfectly natural action on the part of the horse and should be expected. The testing will be mild at first. The horse might just get a little "pushy" and may even threaten a bit just to find out what the person's reaction will be. If not immediately and firmly squelched, the pushing and threatening will escalate rapidly. The longer a person delays putting a stop to this behavior, the more difficult it becomes. If no firm action is taken until the horse becomes a serious and dangerous problem, it is more than likely too late for it to ever be completely eliminated. Even a good, older horse that is properly "mannered" will still occasionally test a person, and every now and again the rider will need to reaffirm his pecking order position. This reaffirmation is perfectly acceptable in the natural order of things and something a horse fully understands and readily accepts. What the horse is not capable of understanding is being physically punished for violating some arbitrary human rule or value that doesn't exist in the horse world.

For example, a horse that is tied may become startled and, as is common, pull back hard and destroy a very expensive silver-mounted show halter. Then, as is also common, when the horse is finally caught, its handler will give it a severe whipping. Since time and money don't exist in the horse world, any punishment in this situation only serves to create confusion, fear, and mistrust. A horse can, however, understand full well that there will be consequences if it initiates open rebellion or becomes physically aggressive toward a superior in the natural pecking order. When physical punishment is warranted, it must be administered immediately and with force in proportion to the action displayed by the horse. It should leave absolutely no doubt in the horse's mind that there are specific bounds for which there is zero tolerance. It must be carried out quickly enough and with enough force to surprise the horse and cause it to back down, for which it should then be praised. Should the person back down before the horse does, the horse will assume it has rearranged the pecking order, established its dominance, and it will become even more aggressive. A half a ton of lightning-quick, aggressive, powerful muscle can be very intimidating and dangerous, so bear in mind – *and this cannot be emphasized enough* – any situation that honestly calls for physical punishment is not something for the timid, the faint-hearted, or the inexperienced to attempt. Again, this cannot be emphasized strongly enough.

I will relate an experience I had several years ago that, from the opposite end of the issue, illustrates what I've just been talking about. Very early in my horse experience I learned that allowing a horse to "harmlessly nibble" would nearly always lead to far more serious and potentially dangerous biting. To shorten a long story, I discovered that if it was firmly established in the horse's mind early on that a harmless nibble resulted in unwanted consequences, biting never became an issue. I found that the earlier in a horse's life this was established the easier it was accomplished. Ideally, the lesson should be taught before a horse is even a week old.

I learned that by putting a mare and her foal in a large stall with me just sitting in a corner, the foal's natural curiosity was aroused. The foal would hide behind mother at first, but it would keep watching me and get braver and braver until it would finally stick its nose out to smell this strange creature sitting in the corner. As long as I didn't move a muscle the foal would finally grow brave enough to give me a close inspection. As long as all the foal did was sniff and smell, I wouldn't move. Sniffing and smelling are how a horse naturally gathers a lot of information. However, the very first time the foal opened its lips to nibble I would quickly give its nose one solid, open-handed smack, and then continue to sit motionless in the corner.

121

The foal would naturally panic and hide behind mother again, but the curiosity factor in a horse is extremely strong. Before long, maybe five or ten minutes, the foal would very cautiously work its way back to me to continue its investigation. This whole scene might be repeated two or three times, but eventually the foal would figure out that it could give me a complete going over with its nose, and as long as it didn't open its lips I would remain completely motionless and allow it to investigate. From that day forward that horse would never have to be disciplined for biting.

Now, let's flip the coin and look at the other side. One day, as the manager and trainer of a fairly large breeding and showing operation, I was doing this with a foal that was only a few days old. My employer and owner of the facility happened by and stopped to watch. Everything was fine until I smacked the foal on the nose. That poor woman nearly exploded. In no uncertain and very graphic terms I was informed that if I was to ever strike any of her horses for any reason, I would be fired and reported to the authorities for animal cruelty. It seemed to really surprise her when I asked for my pay and quit on the spot. She demanded to know why I was quitting, and I explained that she and everyone else would hold me responsible for her ill-mannered horses.

Now, let's do a little analysis of what happened here. The owner's reasoning went something like this: It's only a baby. It doesn't even have any teeth yet, and it was only nibbling. It doesn't know any better and didn't mean any harm. I have no argument with those facts. They are all true enough. But at just what point in its life does a horse suddenly "know better," and how does it learn?

Let's take a look at how a lot of people tend to deal with a horse of any age that exhibits a tendency to nibble or even just lay its ears back and show mild irritation toward a person. At first the person usually speaks sharply and loudly enough to surprise the horse into backing off. Of course, the horse very quickly learns there are no real consequences for doing what it did other than a loud noise, so it ignores the verbal noise and gets more insistent. The horse rapidly progresses to the point of quickly thrusting its nose toward the person and taking a "nip." What do you suppose the horse is learning from all this? When things have escalated to this point, it is common for a person, not wanting to be cruel or mean to his horse, to continue loudly reprimanding the horse while *pushing* its nose away every time it tries to nip him. Oh, sure, a person will push it hard, very hard. He or she might even give the horse a very light smack on the neck, but there are still no serious or painful consequences. Since the horse understands full well the consequences will be weak, it simply gets progressively sneakier and more adept at avoiding the progressively harder pushes and "love pats." Before long the nipping becomes more aggressive and finally escalates to biting. Only when things reach this point do the pushes become hard smacks which, by then, do absolutely no good because by now this activity has become something of a game for the horse, and it becomes a chronic, sneaky, vicious biter. The horse was very effectively and incrementally "taught" how to duck, dodge, and evade in order to bite people. The fact that this teaching was inadvertent and unintended doesn't matter a whit to the horse, nor does it make its bites less painful. For the rest of its life the horse will be punished often and hard for biting and, in all likelihood, it will badly hurt a few people. Under these circumstances, do you think the "blame" for biting lies with the horse or with the human? I can tell you this, for the foal I taught to not even nibble before it was a week old, biting will probably never be an issue the rest of its life. Which way do you think is in the best long term interests of both horse and human?

Actually what I was doing with the foal was pretty much in line with something much of the horse world has advocated in the last few years: imprinting. Imprinting is the practice of handling a foal as early as possible, preferably from the moment it is born. The theory is that exposing it to human handling and scent as early as possible "imprints" in its brain that humans are a normal part of its world and not to be feared. As early as was practical I was "imprinting" in the foal's brain that it was in its own best interests to keep its mouth shut around people.

Physical punishment timed right and done correctly is very much in line with the way horses communicate amongst themselves, and it plays an important part in any horse/human relationship. Figuring out why and when to punish is not especially difficult, but what about carrying it out correctly? This is where things can get murky and why the inexperienced need to be extremely careful about attempting it. If not done correctly, punishment will, at best, cause more problems than are prevented and, at worst, create a very dangerous situation so fast it is unbelievable. This is precisely why the pros just don't want to talk about it. Punishment involves a large amount of social (and possibly even legal) liability they simply cannot afford to risk and for which they can't be faulted, either.

So, just what is the correct way to punish? First, the punishment needs to be meted out immediately and firmly at the very first indication of any potentially dangerous act. The threat of aggression can be permanently stopped. Biting and kicking, once learned, are forever. As a young man I was told that what I would teach my horses wouldn't be nearly as important as what I didn't allow them to learn. Human or animal, once something is learned it is never unlearned.

When a competent, experienced horseman determines a good, sharp smack is warranted, it is administered immediately (almost instinctively) and with enough force that the horse is "taken aback" in surprise. There is roughly a three second window of opportunity if the punishment is going to be effective. Waiting even ten seconds after the fact is enough time that the horse will not be able to associate what it did with the punishment it is receiving, and the punishment will only serve to produce confusion, fear, and mistrust in the horse. Because it won't have any idea why it is being punished, you are better off doing nothing at the time but "setting them up" for it later when you are prepared and can do it right.

Whether the punishment is the open hand or a riding crop, it should be one, *and only one,* good, sharp smack. The smack should be hard enough to "leave no doubt in the horse's mind that it overstepped its bounds." If a second smack (or more) is applied, any positive effect the first one had will be completely undone and the horse will either want to just run away or become defensive and dangerously aggressive. One sharp smack will surprise the animal and obtain its full attention. If done quickly enough, the horse will simply accept it as the undesirable and preventable consequence of whatever aggressive action it displayed. The real trick here is in determining in a split second whether the horse is purposely testing you or is scared and feels threatened and is acting according to its natural instincts.

An aspect of this subject that is often not considered is whether an aggressive action on the part of the horse is some natural, instinctive reaction to something a person has unknowingly or unintentionally done. For example, a horse cannot begin to understand being punished for taking defensive action when a person attempts to clean an open wound with alcohol. It doesn't matter that this is being done for the horse's own good. The wound hurts and defensive action is perfectly normal and should be expected. It is up to the person to understand this and to see that the horse is restrained first. A horse doesn't deserve punishment for a natural reflex action. To kick is very often a perfectly normal reflex when a horse is startled, so is breaking all bonds and running away at all cost when it is scared. These are not punishable events.

This business of teaching what are called "good manners" to a horse is not a simple thing. This is why it is a serious mistake for a novice to purchase a young, untrained horse or, even worse, to attempt to raise one from a baby. Doing so is almost a 100% sure-fire formula for disaster. The end result is almost always everything the novice does not want, and a horse that carries many a bad or dangerous fault with it for the rest of its life.

No matter the circumstances, whenever you are dealing with a horse there are no simple, clear-cut procedures that will work every time without fail. Horses do not function like machines. This is why it is so important to understand the nature of the horse and to develop the ability to communicate *with* the horse on its level. Only when you are able to ask your horse for something in a manner it can understand is it going to respond in a consistent, predictable, positive, and safe manner. That's also when horse and rider truly become a team and, for all appearances, think and function as a single unit.

"Back Off!"

(Photo of Concho by C.L. "Lee" Anderson)

Notes

THIRTEEN

The Bottom Line

Every move a horse makes *should* be telling its rider something. Whether intended or not, every move a rider makes *is* telling the horse something. The plain and simple fact is that it is impossible for anyone's level of horsemanship to exceed their ability to communicate with their horse. There are an abundance of very good trainers today doing things with horses that seem to defy explanation. Almost without exception, these horsemen are more than willing to explain and demonstrate how they go about achieving their extraordinary skills. People unconsciously assume that by following their examples and explanations to the letter, they can accomplish what the pros do.

Many of these good horsemen put on well-attended clinics and seminars for just this purpose. However, if one listens closely to what the trainers say, their primary message often centers on what equipment to use and how to properly use it. I have yet to hear even one of these trainers adequately explain *why* the equipment works (or doesn't work) from the horse's standpoint. The audiences assume that since these people are nationally known, high-profile, big time show ring winners and moneymakers, whatever they say is absolute gospel, and people are convinced the equipment is going to be the "silver bullet" that will give them the same results. Many do purchase the equipment (which the trainer is often paid to endorse or just happens to own the marketing rights for) and attempt to apply it exactly as they were told and shown. Unfortunately, very few ever achieve the same results they saw demonstrated at the clinic. Most will end up disappointed, and quite a few just figure the professional is simply keeping a lot of secrets to protect his livelihood.

In today's technologically advanced world, from the day we are born we are literally "brainwashed" into assuming that some piece of advanced technology can substitute for a skill that would otherwise take years to develop. This may be true enough when dealing with problems in the electro-mechanical world, but nothing could be farther from the truth when dealing with a horse. If skilled enough, a person can do almost anything with a horse with nothing but skill. Every piece of equipment should be considered as nothing more than an aid, not a substitute for skill. Nothing has ever, nor will ever, substitute for skill when working with a horse.

Now, don't misinterpret me. These professionals are, without question, extremely good at what they do and are more than willing to share whatever they know. The question is, are they actually cognizant of all the subtle, underlying reasons for *why* what they do works? I question this because few people are skilled analysts. Ask any computer programmer how well people can explain to them, step-by-step, exactly how they perform their jobs. Even if someone is a pretty good analyst, are they articulate enough to explain it in a way the average horse owner can understand?

Most assuredly these trainers are good at what they are doing, which is primarily winning ribbons and championships in the highly competitive show ring or conducting financially successful clinics. What the average horse owner needs to understand and accept is that the show ring is just that and nothing more – a show. It is also the foundation on which the business side of today's horse world rests. This very often means the winner needs to be more showman and businessman than horseman. Actual show ring performance is subject to the whims, fancies, and motives of those who make the rules. The clothing a rider wears has nothing whatsoever to do with how well a horse performs or the rider rides. However, the "correct" clothing is plainly laid out in the rules and strictly enforced. The logical conclusion has to be that more than one show ring rule exists to help the judges eliminate exhibitors on nit-picking rule violations rather than the promotion of good, solid, fundamental horsemanship.

Not many things are more frustrating than to have your horse put on a flawless performance but lose any chance at a ribbon because the rules call for some totally irrelevant piece of gear (hobbles, a rope, a quirt, chaps, type of bit or reins) and you overlooked it.

Keeping the show moving in a timely manner plays a big part in the overall show ring picture. The total difference between first and last place in a national championship class of twenty-five horses couldn't be measured with an electron microscope. Without some way to quickly eliminate most of the competitors, the time it would take to properly judge the class could stretch into hours, if not days.

There are those who argue that showmanship isn't a factor in the timed events such as barrel racing. To a certain extent that is true because an inanimate electronic timer determines who wins. The problem here, however, is that few horses that are consistent winners in these events are good all-around performers. Their training is highly specialized with a very narrow focus. There are, of course, exceptions to everything I've stated, but they are extremely rare.

Compare the way a racecar is equipped with the way the average automobile in rush hour traffic on the freeway is equipped and why. That's not unlike the world of difference between competing in the show ring and good, solid, everyday horsemanship.

Please don't take this to mean I think the show ring is bad, because it isn't. On the contrary, it can be a source of a great deal of pleasure, enjoyment, and even income. It is a terrific ego pump to be awarded first place whether it's a ribbon at a small-town fun show or a championship trophy at the national level. Just don't confuse what it takes to win in the show ring with good horsemanship because they are not necessarily the same thing. It's the old "apples to oranges" comparison. The only thing they have in common is that both are delicious fruits.

To achieve a national championship, a person's efforts have to be focused on nothing beyond achieving absolute perfection within the limited scope of the rules under which the animal will be competing. This is often a very narrow scope, and everything outside of that scope is virtually ignored, making the horse pretty much useless otherwise. If you think differently, take any average racehorse right off the track and take it on a trail ride.

Speaking of trail riding, many a horse that can win a trail class in the show ring would be a miserable, if not outright dangerous horse on an honest-to-goodness trail ride in the great outdoors. I tell you this from first-hand experience. The show ring and the sort of training it requires are a far cry from everyday, real life.

What this boils down to is this: if you intend to produce show ring winners, be prepared to compromise some of the rules of good horsemanship. This does not, however, in any way lessen the need to understand how to effectively communicate with your horse. It simply means your communicating will be done with a different purpose and have a far different end result. The methods of communication are still going to be the same because no horse can act or respond contrary to its nature no matter what your goal. Outside of the fancy trappings and the number of spectators, a horse sees little difference between a show ring and a training arena. They are both an interruption to its day.

Sifted down to the bottom line, no matter what the goal, be it a trail horse, pleasure horse, reining horse, cutting horse, parade horse, a hunter or jumper, an "eventor," dressage horse, or even just a backyard pet, your level of success depends solely on how well you and your horse are able to communicate *with* each other.

What's been related in this book isn't rocket science by any stretch of the imagination. Just because a person doesn't understand something doesn't mean it's magic. Where a horse is concerned, dealing with it involves a lot of common sense coupled with knowledge and an awareness of the nature of the animal and how it interprets the things around it along with what you do. Handling a horse well has a great deal to do with building a solid bond of trust and respect between the two of you. It involves making the horse a partner and a friend rather than a slave.

Now, how about you get out there and have a long, serious talk with your horse.

HORSES THAT HELPED ME ALONG THE WAY

Old Beauty, a horse my mother rode as a youngster and who taught me to ride when I was eight-years-old

Mabel replaced Old Beauty when she passed on

Blondie, my first *real* horse

Princess, who could win a pole bending one minute and a kid's pleasure class the next

Mr. War Leo, the first reining horse I trained

Fly Hancock, the quickest three-year-old I ever tried to mount (it took two failed attempts).

Hillcrests Imarka, the first stallion I trained and the number two trail horse at the Arabian National Finals in 1965

Imaress, the offspring of Hillcrest Imarka and Princess and greatly admired by Vern Danielson

Two D Two, a wonderful ride and the first cutting horse I rode

Duck and Run, the gutsiest horse I ever rode

Two Eyed Jack, a big, clumsy two-year-old that went on to become a world champion and a legend

Negam, an Arabian stallion who was the meanest, most untrustworthy horse I ever worked with

Flis, a bold, magnificent Arabian stallion that scared the hell out of everyone but me

Count Flis, who was sired by Flis and who I rode 100 miles in 19 ½ hours

Czarnyen, the homeliest and _the_ best working Arabian I ever rode

Dusty, a race track rescue and a veritable equine ballet dancer, now retired

Concho, my current mount, a race track rescue, a bridle horse, and a best buddy

There are an untold number of other horses I worked with over the years whose names I can't remember.

I learned something from every one of them.

About the Author

Lee Anderson grew up in a small town in central Iowa farm country in the 1940s and '50s and relocated to Arizona in the 1970s. Before Lee was out of diapers he showed an intense interest horses. As he grew a little older he took every opportunity to ride or work with any horse its owner would allow. When Lee was about eight-years-old, his father made arrangements for him to have the pony his mother had ridden when she was a youngster. Lee's been on a horse since.

Early on Anderson found that a horse could be taught many things. Lee would read anything that concerned horses and hung out with as many horse people as he could. He soaked up horse information like a sponge and couldn't get enough of it. His mother always said he was a walking encyclopedia of unimportant facts.

When Lee was sixteen his buddies just knew he'd lost every bit of what little good sense he had. They were trying to scrape together $60 or $70 for some old car, and Lee went and spent $150 of his own money on a horse. A few years later when their cars were junk, Lee sold his horse for $200!

After a few years of college, Lee started training show horses professionally. He did more training than showing, but he managed to show the number two Arabian Trail Horse at the Arabian National

Finals in 1964. That's also about the time he lost all interest in competing and was satisfied just to work with his own horses for the pleasure of it and to learn as much as he could about the nature of horses and how to use that nature to his advantage.

Over the years Lee watched how people dealt with horse issues. While most folks did all right, very few ever achieved a good, solid understanding of why their horses did or didn't do things. He noticed that, more often than not, most horse issues are approached from the person's point of view, but the horse can only respond according to its nature and from its point of view. Sadly, there's a lot of distance between the two views. Anderson spent well over half a century studying what makes horses do what they do and how to modify that behavior without resorting to man-handling the horse. At the urging of his wife, Margaret, and several friends, Lee attempted to put some of what he'd learned in written form. It's his sincere hope that this book can help both people and horses.

Publisher Note:

Our sincere thanks to Allen Patrou for his graciousness and generosity in allowing us to use his award-winning photo of Lee and Concho for our cover and also for the interior photo of Lee and Concho. Patrou, a resident of Arizona, is a multi-award-winning photographer. You can learn more about this outstanding artist and see examples of his work at www.aptrouphotography.com.

We also wish to thank Barb Pritchard (aka Tumbleweed Tillie) for the use of her photos. www.backintymephotos.com.

Recent Moonlight Mesa Publications

Western:

Jere D. James: The Jake Silver Adventure Series-
Saving Tom Black, 2009
Apache, 2010
Canyon of Death, 2011
High Country Killers, 2012

Paula L. Silici: *A Way in the Wilderness*, 2011

R.L. Coffield, Compiler: *Award-Winning Tales*, 2011

Stoney Greywolf Bowers: *Reflections from the Wilderness*, 2009
(Cowboy Poetry)

J.R. Sanders: *The Littlest Wrangler*, 2010 (Award-Winning Young
Reader for ages 7 – 10)

Jonah Arizona: *Sam's Desert Adventure*, 2012 (Young Reader for
ages 7 – 11)

Nonfiction:

Rusty Richards: *Casey Tibbs – Born to Ride*, 2010

Becky Coffield: *Life Was A Cabaret – A Tale of Two Fools, A Boat and a Big-A** Ocean*, 2005 (Award-Winning)

C.L. "Lee" Anderson: *Developing the Art of Equine Communication*, 2012

Suspense:

R.L. Coffield: The Ben Thomas Trilogy
Northern Escape, 2005 (Award-Winning)
Northern Conspiracy, Book II, 2011
Death in the Desert, Book III, 2009